ALEXANDRA CHAURAN

GETTING
THROUGH IT

© Sarah O'Brien

About the Author

Dr. Alexandra Chauran (Port Moody, BC) is a second-generation fortune-teller, a high priestess of British Traditional Wicca, and the queen of a coven. As a professional psychic intuitive for over a decade, she serves psychic apprentices and thousands of clients. She received a master's degree in teaching from Seattle University and a doctorate from Valdosta State University and is certified in tarot. In her spare time, she can be found streaming poker at http://www.twitch.tv/queenofdiamonds.

ALEXANDRA CHAURAN

GETTING
THROUGH IT

RECLAIM & REBUILD Your Life After
ADVERSITY, CHANGE, or TRAUMA

Llewellyn Publications
Woodbury, Minnesota

FIRST EDITION
First Printing, 2020

Book design by Lauryn Heineman
Cover design by Shira Atakpu
Cover illustration by James Steinberg / Gerald & Cullen Rapp
Interior illustrations by Llewellyn Art Department

Llewellyn Publications is a registered trademark of Llewellyn Worldwide Ltd.

Library of Congress Cataloging-in-Publication Data
Names: Chauran, Alexandra, author.
Title: Getting through it : reclaim & rebuild your life after adversity,
    change, or trauma / [Alexandra Chauran].
Description: First edition. | Woodbury, Minnesota : Llewellyn Publications,
    [2020] | Includes bibliographical references. | Summary: "Having battled
    life-threatening illness and gone through a complicated divorce, former
    hospital chaplain Alexandra Chauran has spent years developing the best
    strategies for getting through incredible hardships. In this book she
    shares personal stories and proven techniques for healing and handling
    trauma"— Provided by publisher.
Identifiers: LCCN 2020028157 (print) | LCCN 2020028158 (ebook) | ISBN
    9780738764207 (paperback) | ISBN 9780738766560 (ebook)
Subjects: LCSH: Grief. | Loss (Psychology) | Psychic trauma. | Healing. |
    Self-help techniques.
Classification: LCC BF575.G7 C46267 2020 (print) | LCC BF575.G7 (ebook) |
    DDC 155.9/3--dc23
LC record available at https://lccn.loc.gov/2020028157
LC ebook record available at https://lccn.loc.gov/2020028158

Llewellyn Publications
A Division of Llewellyn Worldwide Ltd.
2143 Wooddale Drive
Woodbury, MN 55125.2989
www.llewellyn.com

Printed in the United States of America

Also by Alexandra Chauran

*My biggest achievement in life
has been the privilege to touch the very inner hearts of
some of the very best people on this earth.*

Contents

Introduction

J

Learning that you have a serious life upheaval will come with a great deal of grief. You will need to grieve the future that you could have had if you did not have to rebuild your life from scratch. You may need to grieve even more things. For example, I lost my breasts and my ovaries in the fight against breast cancer, and I had to grieve those losses as well as the fallout in my social and romantic life that resulted from those losses. Since life marches on regardless of whether or not you're mired in a problem, you may also find yourself grieving the loss of a home, a job, a friend, or a marriage. This book is organized in the famous Kübler-Ross model of the stages of grief: denial, anger, bargaining, depression, and acceptance. Each of these stages applies to losses you may be experiencing at the beginning of each section. I used Kübler-Ross because this model is so pervasive in our culture that I, and many of my cancer peers, have found ourselves worrying and wondering how we fit into the model and whether we're progressing through it somehow in the right way. I also found that others around me were aware of the popular model for grief and expected the stages to come from me in a certain order and then for me to just get over it.

The Kübler-Ross model of the stages of grief may not be scientifically accurate, but many do experience a spiraling through the emotions associated with the model, gaining a new perspective each time they go through them. As you feel the emotions associated with your illness, you don't have to work through the book in order. Flip to the section of the book that deals with the feelings you're experiencing right now, or flip to the section on tools for healing from your losses or finding your new normal when you're in the right headspace to move forward with practical solutions. Keep a journal of what you've done and what you have yet to do. Don't be tricked by your own mind into thinking that you haven't had some of these feelings if you know that you're the type who typically stuffs feelings down deep inside. For example, I often ignore my own sadness, preferring to distract myself with something else. Unfortunately, ignoring the blues does not allow me to process through them and move beyond the problem that has been plaguing me.

In the latter half of the book, some important issues to warriors surviving all sorts of life challenges, from single parenting to surviving cancer, are explored. Yes, this book is about keeping positive in the face of something bleak and horrible, but you also will need many coping mechanisms for when positivity simply cannot be constant. A section on recovering your strength of body, mind, spirit, or all three if they are available to you is included. I'm, of course, not qualified to diagnose or treat any disease, so I hope that you're already working with a qualified medical team if physical healing is your goal. We'll explore both traditional and alternative methods of emotional, spiritual, or physical healing, which I believe can coexist and complement one another, from whatever neutron bomb hit your life.

Finally, this book will end with a discussion on finding your new normal. Things may never be able to return to what they were before, but starting right now you can begin building a future that can include the infinite joys of a moment spent in the here and now.

A LITTLE ABOUT ME

Since you'll be reading bits and pieces of my journey as personal examples throughout this book, I'd like to give you a brief back-story here so that you can understand the timeline of events. I haven't lived my entire life jam-packed with adversity. I just had a rough two and a half years. My childhood was pleasant and rich with love and adventure. As a young adult, I learned to cope as best as one can with mental illness and discovered that I had a kidney disease that could prove fatal, but not for a few decades. Thankfully, I was supported by loved ones and was able to keep some semblance of a normal life and emotional outlook.

The real traumas were set off with a bang in December 2014, when a truck crossed the double-yellow line and struck my car head-on. For a while, I couldn't walk unassisted, and I battled a phobia of driving. After I had nearly fully healed from that traumatic event, in 2015 I was diagnosed with high-risk breast cancer. I endured five months of chemotherapy while caring for my small children. In 2016 I had double mastectomies, had thirty-six radiation treatments, and lost my fertility when my ovaries were removed. Four weeks after my last surgery, the husband I had been with for fourteen years disappeared with a friend of mine. I was forced to move all our belongings into storage and sell our home. I left to stay at a friend's home with only the possessions that could fit in my small car. What followed was a plunge into a brutal year of legal battles. Though I had remained cheerful throughout cancer treatment, the divorce, with all its lies and betrayals, made me feel like cancer had taken everything from me and that my inner light had been snuffed out.

Up until then, I had only witnessed tragedy from the outside. I had been a hospital chaplain, witnessing many awful life transitions. I was there offering hugs when families were first informed of a loved one's death. I baptized babies that wouldn't live more than minutes. I had to explain to a small child who had just survived a terrible car accident why she wouldn't see Mommy and Daddy ever again, having to answer questions as the four-year-old struggled to understand that they weren't sleeping or mad at her. I squeezed the hand of a rape victim as she attempted to relive horrific details for police inquiries. I prayed with an elderly woman who had been screaming Hail Marys for hours after a traumatic brain injury, and I chatted quietly about hope with a man who had been stuck in hospital for years due to a persistent case of tuberculosis. My clinical pastoral education training could only partially prepare me for what experience has taught. I also hold a master's degree in education, which helped me write this book as a series of teachings that build on one another. Thank you for trusting me as your guide on your journey.

By 169 days after diagnosis, I was declared "no evidence of disease," the closest they get to calling somebody cured of cancer. If I am honest with myself, I can say that cancer treatment and its aftermath were the worst years my life. However, I still laughed frequently, hugged my loved ones, formed new allies, and gained wisdom and perspective that I might otherwise never have received until old age. But this book isn't necessarily about getting "cured" of any malady. The exercises will help you heal from the trauma of experiencing any terrible chapter of life, such as a health crisis of your own or of a loved one, divorce, death of a loved one, losing a job, losing your home security, or any other nasty thing that life throws at you. Keep in mind that you or a loved one can experience healing from serious physical illness, even if that means having to come to a place of peace with a very dire prognosis. Although my prognosis is now bright, recovering from the disease and its effects on my life and the lives of those around me hasn't been all sunshine and rainbows. One can be healed and still suffer just as one can die happily far too early.

Chapter 1

J

DUELING WITH DENIAL

Denial is often the first reaction to horrible news. We clutch our hair. We scream no into the night. We lie in bed in the morning and soak up that beautiful moment before reality hits that life has irrevocably changed.

If you are stuck crying out that you are not ready for what is happening to you, do not fear. You don't have to understand absolutely everything right now and in this moment. Death, love, loss, and the question of why bad things happen to good people are all mysteries that have befuddled philosophers for centuries. Reach out to spiritual resources and reach inward to begin to formulate your own understanding.

While your world might seem to be falling apart, the rest of the world keeps moving right along. You might notice that others around you seem to be jumping ahead in life while you stand still. Births and deaths and weddings may mark time, and, yes, the sun will continue to rise even if your life has been forever changed. You might find yourself feeling deep envy of others who seem to be enjoying life, or you might simply feel a sense of odd confusion. How can others move on with life when you've lost your own world?

Life does move on, and there's no way that you can put a hold on other areas of life while you fight your battles. Grief and healing do not proceed in an orderly manner, one right after the other. If you find that your life problems and feelings are all mixed up, you are not alone. There will be times when life moves slowly and other times when misfortunes come in groups.

Daniel was a friend of mine who was a mechanic happily married to his high school sweetheart, Carrie. Life was good, except that their teenaged son Johnathan was with a girlfriend they didn't approve of. It was a minor disagreement in the family, though Carrie suspected that the girlfriend was on drugs. One spring day, Daniel came home to his son standing in the living room. "I think I killed Mom," Johnathan said, in a moment that Daniel would relive in his head for the rest of his life. In the ensuing chaos, Daniel saw some horrible sights that he'd hoped he would never see. Unable to sleep in the house he had lived in with his family, Daniel slept in his mechanic's shop that night. His relationship with his son was forever changed, if not destroyed, and he couldn't fathom a world without Carrie in it. Nobody could have predicted his son's actions. There had been no red flags.

Cancer also had come to me from the clear blue sky. I was thirty-four years old with no family history of young cancer. I ate a healthy diet, was a marathon runner, breastfed my two children, and had never been overweight a day in my life. Not that those other lifestyle choices are bad, but they can all be risk factors for breast cancer. I was the last person that people in my immediate social circle thought would develop such a devastating disease. I was also blindsided by the subsequent divorce, having willfully ignored the signs two months before my husband left. I know I'm not alone in life's surprising events. My friend came home one day to find her partner gone, having left all his belongings behind. She was terrified that something awful had happened to him, and in the following months it became known that he had simply left without saying a word after years of living together. They never spoke again. She held on to his belongings for many years, hoping to at least speak to him once more.

Chances are, most people reading a self-help book such as this have a natural intuition. Why, then, are intuitive people surprised by big life changes that are forced upon them? Nobody is ready for some life events until they happen. Many are not ready to have children until they have them, but they do rise to the challenge. Even after taking parenting classes before giving birth, there's nothing like the real thing.

Shock and denial are often a part of the grief process and nearly always a piece of any great transition. Your illness or dark time in your life can be a catalyst to learn some new coping mechanisms for dealing with denial. One thing that has changed about me since cancer is that when I hear bad news, instead of spending too much time saying, "No, no, no, no!" I can simply tell myself, "Well, this is happening." Skipping the part where you fight against life can be a welcome relief, but if you're not quite there yet, never fear. This chapter will give you some gentle help to guide you through any period of shock.

HOW TO ASK FOR HELP AND HOW DENIAL AFFECTS RELATIONSHIPS, FAMILY, AND HOME LIFE

Put Yourself First and Be Realistic about Your Ability to Help Others

You're not a bad person if you're not helping others right now. This is so important that I feel the need to repeat it by restating it in another way: if you are unable to give back to the people who are giving to you, or to otherwise meaningfully contribute to your community right now, it is not your fault or your failing. The same person who wants to help others is still inside you right now.

As a helper personality, Lisa was always trying to give all of herself away. She worked hard for her children, her husband, and for whatever was the latest volunteer cause she'd undertaken. After an autoimmune disease treatment, she fell into a deep funk. She felt like she wasn't even half the person that she used to be. She was no longer volunteering for a half-dozen causes. She couldn't drag herself out of town to buy groceries for a loved one in need. She felt like she had taken a big step backward in life. She wasn't herself. She wasn't the person that she wanted to be. If you feel like Lisa did, you're not alone.

It's likely that if you are feeling pressure to help others right now, you might be putting that pressure on yourself. Allow yourself the same grace that you would allow to a friend who was going through hardship. You are still the same person. Your new motto: Start with attention before action. When I struggled to take on a role to help others, I found myself teaching a meditation class to my own cancer support group. Soon, I found myself unable even to make the barest commitment to teaching regular meditation classes, as I struggled to put my life together in the immediate aftermath of cancer. Of course, my cancer friends and my social worker understood that I wanted to help, and they didn't put any pressure on me.

Reconnecting with Family as Relationships Change

The gravity of how your social landscape may change cannot be overstated. I saw divorce, the loss of friendships, and the permanent shifting of power dynamics within my family because of illness. I know that my young children had their formative years shaped by my experience with cancer and its treatment, and they will never be the same. A friend of mine even saw a dramatic disappearance in friends after she gave birth to triplets, which should have been a joyous occasion to gather people together. It may be difficult to see the loss of relationships as a positive, but serious illness can be a crucible for positive change.

Whenever you think of a question to ask someone in your family, try not to wait until the next time that you happen upon that family member, and instead reach out to him or her immediately. Family bonding springs from hard times. After people who I trusted the most seemingly abandoned me, my therapist suggested that I start by trusting only family members and proceed from there. I picked up the phone and called my cousins, with whom I hadn't spoken in quite a long time. Before cancer, I held some family members at arm's length. There was always some other time to talk with distant relatives. After serious illness, however, I am more cognizant that my days are numbered. Our lives are finite. There's no time like the present to give family members a call.

Ultimately, other people make their own choices, and there is nothing you can do to change their minds if they are insistent about leaving your life. My own experiences are not entirely rare, and I've heard many heartbreaking stories from friends in my cancer support groups about friends and even children who severed ties when a person became sick. I cannot generalize here why some people cannot cope with having a loved one with a serious illness. I know that, in my case, there were certainly other factors at work besides my illness, namely my own coping mechanisms, choices, and attitudes about my illness and life in general, that could have driven some people away. However, I do know that clinging to people who wanted to leave my life only exacerbated the problem and prolonged the suffering of everyone concerned.

Horror Stories

When the brain hears enough horror stories about the world, the nervous system goes on high alert. A person watching enough news stories about tragedy may feel like he is in a war zone. The solution, of course, is to turn off the television or whatever media is feeding that fear. Put yourself on a low-tragedy diet and stop seeking out stories to read about your situation unless they are positive and have a happy ending.

. . . .

Put yourself on a low-tragedy diet and stop seeking out stories to read about your situation unless they are positive and have a happy ending.

. . . .

People can't help but share the horror stories about the worst-case scenarios they've visited. They will tell a newly diagnosed friend countless stories about grandparents, parents, and distant friends who have succumbed to cancer. Some people read detailed news stories about horrible crimes so intently that dastardly acts are soon viewed as epidemic. During my divorce, people told me horror stories of never being allowed to move and of feeling imprisoned by their legal restrictions for the rest of their kids' childhoods. When I wasn't being told these stories by complete strangers in line at the grocery store or by visitors to my own home, I found myself seeking out these stories in books or on the internet. Why do people tell these stories? Why do I listen to them? And, in the end, what can be done?

Getting people to stop telling you the worst things they've ever heard is a little more difficult than turning off a television. People tell these stories in order to relate to you, and paradoxically, to try to tell you how different your case is from somebody else's sad story. Try to short-circuit these stories whenever possible. Sometimes, a simple "Why are you telling me this?" is enough to elicit a pause and an apology. Sometimes, you might have to be direct by saying, "Excuse me, I'm sorry, but I can't hear another sad story right now. It gives me anxiety. Thank you."

You don't necessarily owe anyone your story, either. If you want to share it, be bold and ask for what you want. If you are sharing your struggles for the purpose of asking for help, be concrete about your requests for assistance. If you simply need some emotional support or reassurance, go ahead and ask for those things flat out, rather than verbally dancing around your needs by moping, blaming, or complaining. It can be helpful to seek out alternative points of view, or to find others who share a similar story to yours to gain some perspective.

The Protocol for Help

Here's a specific protocol for offering help. If followed, a lot of arguments can be easily avoided:

Step 1: Ask first, before helping, if the person wants help.

Step 2: If the person says no, do not help the person. If the person says yes, help the person only to the extent that the person wants help. This requires further communication.

For example, if a person is in a wheelchair, it might feel natural to immediately step in and try to help the person with everything, whether it be reaching something on a high shelf or opening the door to her own home. These acts of kindness are certainly well-meaning, but they can reinforce the feeling of disability in somebody who wants to continue to feel capable. Even if you are still in fine physical health and are going through another massive life upheaval, some friends or family members may try to smother you and baby you, just to be helpful. I know that I felt a little frustrated when people attempted to anticipate my needs and walked all over my attempts to contribute to the family.

If you find yourself abnormally frustrated at loved ones who are trying to help, pay attention to whether or not they are adhering to the protocol for help. If one of the steps is only partially acknowledged, offer specific feedback to the culprit. Chances are, he or she can make a small change and still feel like he or she is helping in a good way. For example, if you need some-body to go grocery shopping for you but not take over the pro-cess of making dinner, express those limits clearly, and your helper will be glad to have his or her efforts streamlined.

Meditation: Forgiveness

Forgiveness is not a natural part of everyone's spiritual-ity. Though it is a tenet of some world religions, others stress a fierce sense of personal responsibility. However, you don't need to relinquish your own sense of power in order to let go of a need for retaliation or an impo-tent anger that eats you up inside. Forgiveness, when paired with boundaries so that the slight does not hap-pen again, can be a powerful spiritual tool to free you from an obsession with balancing the scales and making things fair.

For this type of meditation, lie on a bed, on the floor, or outdoors in the grass with your feet together and your arms out and slightly downward, palms up. This is the peace sign, based on semaphore flag signs. Forgiveness isn't easy, because it is a relinquishment of control. First, consider whether you believe in an arbi-ter such as spirit, the universe, or karmic scales. If you can turn things over to this higher power, it will be very useful. Recognize that you are a part of this higher power, and this higher power lives within you. Breathe out deeply and release the imbalance you're holding. In meditation, forgive at least one person, especially if that one person is yourself.

Meditation: Allowing Yourself to See the Best in People

Suspecting the motives of others gets you through life. It's what makes us refuse to hop into the car with every stranger or decide not to give money to that person asking for help over the phone. However, if you have a serious life upheaval, it can be important to make peace with people in your life. You don't need to allow toxic people back into your life if you've rightfully excluded them, but you can rest assured that, in general, most people have your back.

A suspicion that friends are just coming to watch you when you're at your worst or even that doctors care more about buying another round of golf than they do about your health can be extremely detrimental toward your ability to receive help. Begin courageous conversations if you need to. Visualize yourself wrapped in the love of your community, and every time somebody offers you help, allow yourself to imagine them adding to the love that enfolds you. For this meditation, visualize yourself wrapped in ribbons of light that represent the love of each family member, friend, or doctor in your life.

HOW DENIAL AFFECTS WORK LIFE, PLANNING, AND LOGISTICS

Manifestation List

It is okay to dream wildly about the future, even if your future may not match up with your expectations. During treatment, I fantasized about how I would look in my family holiday photos once my hair grew back, smiling as I wondered how long it would grow. I imagined all the trips I would take with my family once I was well. As my treatment ended, I found myself plunged into a divorce that lasted a year and was unable to realize many of my dreams. My holiday photos showed me sporting lovely short hair, but those pics were missing a former family member and a piece of my heart.

Jenna's recovery from a traumatic brain injury lasted five long months. Since her recovery continued through the winter, she found herself fantasizing impatiently about the warm spring and summer to come. She spent the winter in her basement, in a haze and wrapped in blankets, feeling like her life was on pause. She imagined regaining her strength and competing in running competitions again. She vowed to herself that she would go camping again, even though she hadn't camped out in a tent for perhaps a decade.

. . . .

It is never too bleak to dream about the future.

. . . .

Life is full of seasons and cycles. There are some traditions that can be carried on in your life despite the barriers and difficulties that life presents. It is never too bleak to dream about the future.

My therapist asks cancer patients to start making a "manifestation list." I was thankful that she did not use the term *bucket list*. The benefit of making a manifestation list is that one doesn't have to be reasonable about what sorts of things on the list one could complete. You can add all sorts of things to your manifestation list. Some of the items on your list can be interpersonal goals for your family and relationships. You can also list recreational aspirations, travel, or career goals.

Making a manifestation list is therapeutic in several ways. As you write your list, you can envision very clearly what your life might look like if you were to fully recover from your traumatic life events. As I hunkered down for chemotherapy through the winter, it was my own dark winter of the soul. I was happy to imagine traveling to Disneyland in the springtime, which was something that I did with my children the following year. Write your own manifestation list and hang it somewhere prominent, where you will see it often.

Striking a Balance Between Distraction and Reality

We live in a culture of distractions. We multitask by listening to audiobooks while commuting. We tackle housecleaning while playing a hide-and-seek game with children. It can be hard to find fulfillment with and appreciation for life in between the minutiae. As a Gemini, I'm as guilty of multitasking as anyone. Far be it for me to suggest that distractions from life are somehow wasting its precious moments. It is important, however, to be mindful of how much distraction you seek.

If you're shut indoors most of the time, taking a journey to your front step might be enough of an adventure. If you're able to visit friends or family, you might find that the effort is worth it. If all that you can do is meditate and travel in your mind, that is okay as well. A friend of mine, bedbound, said that the deepest bond she ever felt with her husband was when they traveled together to imaginary places in their heads while lying side by side.

A friend of mine loses time to television, which is her guilty pleasure, but she admits that she watches the screen for more hours than she intends. Everyone, whether young or old, able-bodied or otherwise, should live life with intention. Start by making a short list of what you value in life. Even if you can't travel the world right now, if you value adventure, you should be able to dive into a world within a book or read travel reviews if you're looking forward to feeling better soon.

Don't Just Do Something, Sit There

Traditionally, we are asked to avoid waiting around. We are expected to take action. If you're a go-getter, you might find yourself in a bit of a pickle when your life is in crisis. Instead of being able to address issues as they come with careful planning and preparation, you'll find yourself reacting to everything, sometimes overreacting. Sometimes, life can seem a bit like you're a pendulum swinging between two extremes. When you reach the end of motion, you have little time to relax before swinging back to some other extreme. Being able to get used to the situation is not an option. Instead, you must be at peace during times of motion when things in life are speeding up and changing directions at the same time.

In real-life situations, you might have a much slower-moving crisis on your hands, with a dynamic sense of urgency that causes you to act like you're on fire. You may not be as dynamic, cheerful, or able to influence the world in the ways that you once did. Depending on your situation, you might be working toward returning to your former self, or you might be looking to reinvent yourself based on your limitations. No matter what your station in life, you must begin at the beginning and start your life changes and improvements exactly where you are.

Think about your life goals and dreams and how you can modify them to begin working toward them right now in a way that makes sense for your lifestyle. For example, a friend of mine was about to go on a religious mission to a foreign country when she became sick. She was unable to travel for the foreseeable future and felt sad that she was unable to spread the good word about her spirituality with people in faraway places. She soon found herself talking about the Bible with the person next to her in the hospital waiting room, and she became a mentor to her new friend. In this way, my friend was able to carry out her spiritual mission right where she was in life, from the hospital waiting room instead of from a church in another country.

No matter what factors contributed to your situation, nobody deserves to be punished by suffering for past actions, and you don't have to waste your precious time or emotions on blaming yourself. Over the past few years dealing with treatment and its aftermath, I've spent plenty of time feeling sorry for myself, so I can certainly understand how personal value judgments develop. Your family of origin and your past may have led you to make value judgments on yourself based on your situation.

For example, I was raised in a family that looked down on those who had to take medications, especially for mental health reasons. I grew up to believe that I should work hard for money and save it in order to provide for my family for years to come. I was brought up in a nuclear family to believe that marriage should last a lifetime. Due to illness, I found myself disabled such that I was unable to work, was financially strapped so much that I had to spend my savings, and had my marriage and family torn apart. I have spent so much time judging myself for any past actions or personality failings that have led to my life situation. Ultimately, there were many circumstances beyond my control and, more importantly, all judgments are moot because they are unhelpful to progress toward a brighter future.

· ·

All judgments are moot because they are unhelpful to progress toward a brighter future.

· ·

Frankly, if you were a robot and unable to generate feelings about your station in life, you would be better able to coolly assess where you are and plan steps toward where you are going to go. Thankfully, you are human, so you get to feel a lot of emotions that form the flavor of life as you know it. You can still try to view your place in life objectively, without shame, and understand that the person you are today is going to change going forward.

Exercise: An Affirmation Is the Password

Daily affirmations can feel disingenuous and embarrassing. The most cliché method of using affirmations is to stand in front of the mirror and say positive statements to your own face in a clear and determined voice. If you're able to use affirmations in front of the mirror, by all means please do so, as this can be a highly effective method to change your outlook and your life. However, if you look sickly and feel awful, standing at the mirror and proclaiming your own health might just feel wrong, especially if you're out of practice or new to affirmations. Another option is to write out your affirmations and post them around your house. I had a cluster of affirmations on notes posted in the washroom during my treatment. If you feel embarrassed allowing your housemates to see your affirmations, writing out your affirmation as a computer password can be a wonderful option.

You might very well type passwords dozens of times a day for email, banking, online calendars, and messaging. If you change your password to something that represents your affirmation, such as HomeOwnership2030 or H34lthy@H34rt, you might type your affirmation more than you would say it unless you were feeling especially dedicated to daily focused meditations on your affirmations. Set a goal that you will change within a few months and you'll automatically be reminded to update your password for added security as a bonus.

Exercise: Grounding a Panic Attack

Imagine racing to the hospital for what you think is a heart attack due to stress or some kind of illness that involves shortness of breath and tingly sensations all over your body. The emergency room staff diagnose you with anxiety and send you home, asking you to follow up with your regular doctor. You might feel humiliated, as if you didn't just have a "real" medical emergency, but panic attacks are no joke. You're likely going through one of the more stressful periods of life, and you could be prone to panic attacks. At one point I even took a medication that gave me panic attacks. I thought that, since I am not naturally prone to anxiety, I'd be better able to cope with anxiety when it came. I was wrong. In fact, since I haven't been dealing with anxiety on a regular basis my whole life, I was even more confused when anxiety struck and had to learn how to deal with it in bits and pieces.

One method for dealing with a panic attack is by grounding. Grounding can be an exchange between the spiritual energy of the earth and yourself. It can be done through visualization, vigorous exercise, or eating food. Here is a different way to ground, which is by rooting yourself in the here and now. The idea is to notice things with your senses. First, take a deep breath in and out, noticing any scents in your environment and feeling the air moving in and out of your lungs as your chest or abdomen rise and fall. Feel where you are rooted to the earth, whether by your feet on the ground or your bones on a chair. Notice something in the room that you can count, whether it is lights on the ceiling, knots in wood paneling, or books on a shelf. Close your eyes and pick out some sounds around you. Take another deep breath and reassess how you are doing. Repeat as often as necessary. Try grounding yourself by noticing things with your senses once a day.

SELF-CARE AND SPIRITUALITY

Cocooning
In this busy life where it is considered lazy to stay at home, allow yourself as much leeway as possible. If you can get time off

of work, take full advantage of whatever amount of time off you deserve. If you can ask not to attend large family gatherings, you don't have to feel guilty. Stay at home alone and ask others to go without you. You now have the perfect excuse to avoid loud and boisterous parties and to cuddle up with a good book.

My mother calls it "cocooning" when you spend time indoors or very close to home while you are having a hard time. Embrace the fact that you won't be leaving the house and, instead, focus on making your living space comfortable and cozy. Pull out some soft and comfortable blankets and make yourself a nest. Turn on some of your favorite music, even if it's something childish or embarrassing for others to hear. Make comfort foods and beverages.

Allow your favorite people to cocoon right along with you. When I was sick, I lamented the fact that my kids were trapped at home with a sick mom. If I were well, I could have been taking them to the zoo or to some other enriching activity. I felt sad that my three-year-old had spent a third of his life with "lame" cancer mom. A year later, I was shocked to find out that my kids had fond memories of the cancer family experience. Both of them really loved when Mom would make "blanket nests" in the hallway when she was too tired to walk from the bathroom all the way back to bed. The kids would grab their stuffed animals and some books and curl right up next to Mom in the hallway for a story.

What to Think About before Bed

Here are two things that can help you get some rest and get your mind off of things when you go to bed. The first is to simply go through a list of your loved ones and pray for each one in turn, hoping good things for their futures, even if yours is up in the air. The second thing that can help is to take some time during the day to worry and think through all the difficult thoughts so that you won't start thinking about them right before bed. If I spent the day with distractions, I found that the moment I lay down to sleep my mind became active with all my greatest fears. What my brain needed was to mull over the concerns I had. I used to be able to go for a run to think deep thoughts, but since my exercise routine had changed due to physical disability, I ended up needing to devote more time to thoughtful meditation.

Jacob had always been one to fantasize about the future or to think about positive things right before bed in order to get to sleep. The uncertainty caused by his recent heart attack threw him for a bit of a loop. The hospital staff had called it a "widow-maker," and, quite frankly, he was terrified to close his eyes at night for fear of his potential death. He couldn't picture having the retirement party he had planned for next year, mainly because he was unable to work following release from the hospital. Thankfully, Jacob was a spiritual man, and was able to lean on his Bible studies to give him the faith to put his fears into context.

Finding Bits of Happiness

On even the worst days, there can be small blessings. If you find yourself sequestered due to illness or packing up an entire house following the death or departure of a loved one, you might have to search for the tiniest best moments of your day. The best moment of every day might be getting a morning hug from a loved one. If nobody is available to deliver a hug, the first sip of tea in the morning is a close second. Everyone is different. My mom loves a long candlelit bath as her happy time. My stepdad found joy in people-watching, even during the year when he lost a wife and a daughter to unexpected illnesses.

Now is the time to celebrate even your "guilty" pleasures. If you love the suspense of a scratch-off ticket, it doesn't matter how much of a waste of money buying the ticket might be. If a little bit of joy can be added to your life by scratching to win, you might as well stock up for one a day or one a week, whatever you can afford that will keep the experience special. If you enjoy binge-watching television or reading romance novels, indulge in your pastime without shame. When you're not having such a terrible time in life, you'll have plenty of time to be productive and cut back on superfluous hedonism. Chances are, at this stage in your life, you deserve to "waste" a little time.

Of course, it may not be so simple to build little bits of happiness into your life. You might need to adjust your schedule, plan a budget, or even ask for a little help to get the free time or resources that you need. And remember, happiness can be a relative thing. You don't need to despair if you feel like you haven't felt the unbridled ecstasy of childhood in a long while. Find what makes you smile and build from there.

They say laughter is the best medicine. When I volunteered as a hospital chaplain, the hospital at which I worked had a laughter program. Groups of people would get together with a coach and simply laugh big belly laughter. Although the laughter was forced at first, it soon became so contagious that the whole room would be red faced and smiling.

Now, fake laughter might not be your thing, but it is still okay to put things in perspective and laugh at yourself whenever possible. Doctors and nurses appreciate a little gallows humor as well, so I know that I ingratiated myself with many hospital personnel by cracking jokes. I even have a tattoo on my arm of a voodoo doll, which always gets a laugh out of phlebotomists when they go to draw blood.

Many of us feel that we need a certain set of circumstances in life to be happy. As a spiritual person, I fall prey to thinking that I have not achieved enough in this lifetime. Certainly, the spirit world is complex, and there are things like love and family that I want in my life to feel successful. However, I'm still a simple enough creature that I smile at a picture of a cat or laugh when a baby laughs. It's okay to put the big, serious things in life on hold and laugh at something so simple that it might seem foolish.

. . . .

It's okay to put the big, serious things in life
on hold and laugh at something so simple
that it might seem foolish.

. . . .

Children learn a lot through the power of play. Sometimes, kids create scenarios that are like real life in order to address their own hopes and fears. I watched my kids play way too many doctor games while I was sick, because they heard so much about my doctors and sometimes accompanied me on visits to the hospital. It's a shame that adults don't play as often as children. Sometimes, therapists use role-playing as a means to uncover different feelings.

My own therapist used what she calls "sand tray therapy." Using a small sandbox the size of a dinner tray, she allowed me to choose from a wide selection of toys. Some of the toys were humans, some were monsters, some were machines or bits of scenery. I selected each toy carefully and set them up to create a scene. Afterward, my therapist took a photograph of my diorama and sent it to me. The different toys I selected could be analyzed as Jungian symbols, but I found the process itself to be relaxing and fun.

Is there a way that you can invite more play into your life? Whether by building your own sand tray, giving yourself time to enjoy your favorite games, or simply making each improvement in your life a goal-setting game, find a way to play.

Everything Will Be All Right

Affirmations can be greatly comforting, especially when hearing them from the lips of others. If my mom or dad told me that it was all going to be okay, I believed them without question. You don't have to have reassuring parents in order to find a comforting presence within yourself. There are those who believe that if you repeat the outcome you desire so often that you actually believe your own words, your needs and wants will manifest in the real world. It is certainly worth a shot to allow yourself words of comfort, even if you don't believe them yourself. Tell yourself that things will be all right today as many times as you can.

It may be a little cliché to tell yourself to go to your happy place when things get hard. Visualizing a happy place might not eliminate all your pain if medical personnel are sticking needles in your arms or if you're missing somebody or something very special. However, after my therapist instructed me to learn to mentally take myself to my own happy place, I learned that it helped me relax when I couldn't sleep and helped get me through moments of intense bone pain caused by a medication that was helping me regrow blood cells.

First, choose a place that actually exists to be your imaginary happy place. I chose the Seawall in Vancouver, Canada. As you picture yourself in your happy place, choose a hand sign for yourself that will elicit happy memories for you as you get more practiced in this technique: for example, a thumbs-up sign against your chest. Imagine yourself doing a favorite activity in your happy place. Try to involve all the senses. As I visualized jogging along the Seawall, I imagined that it was a warm afternoon, near sunset, after having my belly filled with a delicious lunch. I smelled the sea air and heard the sounds of the boats knocking against the docks and the seagulls calling. I felt my feet pressing into the earth. After enough practice, I could easily call back the state of mind of being in my favorite happy place using my hand sign. The best part about choosing a real location was that, after I recovered from treatment, it was intensely healing and fulfilling to actually jog once again along the Seawall and feel that I had come full circle.

How Much Are Fear and Anxiety Controlling Your Life?

It has happened to everyone at least once: you get your hopes up, only to have them dashed. Maybe you have an ex-lover who you were sure was "the one" or a job interview that seemed to go well, only to have the position snatched out from under you by another applicant. If you're suffering from a life-threatening illness, the stakes may seem much higher, especially when there are setbacks that make you question or throw out your plans entirely.

My cousin was struggling with his career and had put a hold on his creative dreams in order to try to make enough money to survive in Los Angeles. During the time when his creativity was stifled, he realized that ignoring his dreams wasn't going to brighten his life or make them go away. Listening to my cousin describe his own struggles, it became clear that, from the outside looking in, my own decision to refuse to plan for the future until the future became clear was not a healthy one. I decided to dare to dream, and I never looked back. Fears may not simply evaporate. If you have experienced prolonged anxiety unrelated to your situation, you may need some extra help.

If you feel hopeless, give up hope for a better past. You can change your future, but there's no way that you can change decisions that have already passed. You might have a lot of self-blame and regret lurking around in your mind. Perhaps you made some lifestyle choices in your past that hastened the progression of your life problems. There is no sense beating yourself up over past choices. Chances are that there is no way to understand all the factors that led you to your situation today.

. . . .
There is no sense beating yourself up over past choices.
Chances are that there is no way to understand all
the factors that led you to your situation today.
. . . .

At this point, it is fruitless to have regrets about one's past or to wish to return to it. Instead, one must look forward and hope that the best years are still to come. Popular media portrays cancer survivors as wise people who have somehow become better because of their cancer journey. Cancer is described as a "wake-up call" for somebody who may have not fully appreciated life or who had previously made unhealthy lifestyle choices. For me, it felt as if I had taken a few steps backward. My life seemed fine before cancer. I appreciated my life fully before cancer and led a perfectly healthy lifestyle. Conversely, after cancer I struggled to pick up the pieces of my torn and shattered interpersonal relationships and to rebuild my physical strength to its former glory.

A hopeful spiritual perspective that transcends religious denomination is the idea that death and loss are only the beginning of another grand adventure. In some religions, an eternal paradise or exquisite peace awaits after death, while for others a new cycle of life begins. In nature, we can see that death is necessary for regrowth and birth. It may seem like a new kind of denial to focus on the next life or the great beyond when nearing the end of your lifetime, but a spiritual view of the afterlife can bring great peace to many.

Reach out for resources to study the afterlives of faith traditions of your choice. You may be able to read scripture or other spiritual books that feed your soul and give you some hope. If you are physically able to do so, join a spiritual community for fellowship and encouragement. Begin asking important spiritual questions. You might want to start writing out your own feelings about what happens after death or how the divine can help you through your challenges to start sorting out how you feel. I have friends who were confronted by their own fears about going to hell after death and needed some time to let go of fearing the afterlife.

Curse Breaking

"See, this is why I say I am cursed," my friend said. He was standing in a parking lot with a torn grocery bag, a broken bottle of soy sauce spreading in the rain on the asphalt. I threw him a doubtful look. In the span of under three years I had been through a major car accident, a cancer diagnosis, and a brutal divorce, to say nothing of my pre-existing terminal kidney disease. I never decided that I was cursed. Quite to the contrary, I joke that I am like Rasputin and things keep trying to kill me, but I persist and survive. I can point to equally powerful blessings in my life, such as my two beautiful children, my current freedom from cancer, and the wonderful living and educational opportunities I've enjoyed.

Believing a curse has been placed on a person, however, can have a tremendous personal effect. I'm not just talking about somebody whining about being cursed and then feeling sad. There are very tangible effects that can be brought down on your life simply from believing that you are cursed. The placebo effect can heal, or it can hex. It is important to break away from catastrophic thinking, while still keeping your boots grounded in reality. Things don't have to be perfect, but you can still have good days as well as the bad ones. Perform a simple curse-breaking technique by untying any ties or laces on your clothing, praying for freedom from any negative energy, and then visualizing a shielding bubble of energy surrounding and protecting you. Leave an offering at a crossroads.

Meditation: Miracles

Do you want to hold out hope for a miracle? Your friends and family almost certainly will, even if your situation is grim. It can feel like whiplash for your brain to go from betting on a miracle to planning for homelessness, a funeral, or some other disaster. Allow yourself to decide that you're ready to hope for a miracle, if that's what you want. The worst thing that will happen while praying for a miracle is that it doesn't happen, which is likely the same thing that will happen if you don't pray for a miracle.

This exercise is about leaving yourself open to a miracle, or at least not punishing yourself for hoping for the best. If you find yourself fantasizing about a total cure for your problems, allow yourself to go down that imaginary rabbit hole and fully visualize what would happen if your life was completely restored. Open yourself up, symbolically, by stretching your arms out and lifting your chest. See, in your mind's eye, that there is a vortex of spiritual energy in your chest. This is your heart chakra, and visualizing it opening can help open your heart up to accept change. Visualize your heart chakra opening so that you can accept a miracle into your heart.

Exercise: Eraser

Don't you wish that you could erase giant chapters of your own life sometimes? If only certain memories could be deleted entirely. Unfortunately, real-life memories can't be reprogrammed, and there's no way to have a "do-over" of your childhood, your marriage, or the last five years of your life. Even things that are supposed to undo problems, such as divorce, quitting a toxic job, or selling a childhood home, won't give the closure that one might imagine or hope for in those circumstances. The pain, grief, and sometimes regrets linger on for years or a lifetime.

You can symbolically erase the past in a way that allows you to think forward to the future. Try writing down some of the hopes and fears that you had in the past that you'd like to release, and then erase them or burn the page. Hide photos that remind you of times in the past that are emotionally cutting to you right now. You don't have to burn photos, especially if they're the only copies you have. But you also don't have to display photos on the wall if they only cause you heartache every time that you look at them. It might feel like every moment you can think of in your past brings you pain. If so, start over with today. Put new pictures up on the wall that please you, even if they're just of a flower you saw this morning. Symbolically erase or burn old memories that hurt. Then begin celebrating new ones visually in your home.

Charms and Talismans

Start a lucky charm bag or create a talisman to help you feel calm and connected. One of the first magic talismans I made was during the time that my father was undergoing treatment for his cancer. He gladly accepted a "lucky charm" that was a talisman made of the word *abracadabra*, thought to mean "I create as I speak." The word was turned into an inverted triangle by repeatedly writing the word, decreasing the word by one letter with each line, until it was simply a letter *A* at the point. He felt it was lucky enough to take to his appointments and thereby found a sense of calm and connectedness.

Later, during my own treatment, I started a charm bag when I was given amber earrings from a friend but had no way to wear them since I was getting so many MRIs. I added to this charm bag a Baha'i healing prayer coin from my mom and even a burnt-out light bulb from the radiation machine. These tchotchkes allowed me to feel that I was supported by my loved ones and gave me something to sort through while I received my treatments. Over time, I began imbuing them with lucky wishes by pressing them close in my hands as I prayed and visualized myself after recovery.

Exercise: Letting Go of Denial Completely

Letting go of illusions can help you find true stability in your life. When you feel truly ready to let go of all denial and face your challenges head-on, this exercise can help you symbolically make the leap. Remember, you may need to do this exercise more than once as you fall into the pattern of denial again as a protective defense mechanism.

For this exercise, you'll need a permanent marker to depict your true self, a washable marker to color over it with illusion, a piece of cloth or paper, and a bowl of water to wash away all doubt. Take your time when deciding what to draw as your true, core self on the piece of cloth or paper. You can draw a representation of spirit, or some aspect of your personality that you've had since childhood that you know will endure. Allow the permanent ink to dry completely. Then, draw over your true self with the washable ink to represent illusion. You can just scribble over it completely, or you can draw an artistic representation of your denial. When you are ready, meditate on your true self while gazing into the bowl of water. Then, gently dip the paper or cloth into the water and wash away the illusion. Meditate on this mantra: "Every day I am more and more becoming my authentic self."

Chapter 2

J

ANGER AT THE WORLD

We think of anger as infantile and impotent at best, and dangerous at worst. The very words we use to explain anger, *explosive* and *fiery* for instance, represent how much we loathe to touch it. When dealing with anger, we are asked to "cool off." My fiancé likes to avoid saying that he is angry at all, opting instead for words like *frustrated*. Very rarely do we describe anger as it really is: energizing and motivating. Anger is a natural human emotion, and it can be very valuable as a teaching tool, an outlet for pent-up negativity, and a way to protect and defend yourself.

Recognize when you are feeling angry and try not to stifle your feelings. Instead, observe the anger as if you were on the outside of yourself looking in. Try not to judge your anger. There is nobody on this planet who doesn't "deserve" to be angry. On the other hand, anger is not a reward for being an adequate victim. Allow yourself to feel the anger without stuffing it down deep inside. Find appropriate outlets for your rage and recognize that, when you are feeling anger, there is probably an underlying reason that needs to be addressed. That said, understand also that the anger itself is not a poor reflection on you and it is not its own problem that needs to be solved as quickly as possible. It is possible and okay to be angry for a significant period without it destroying your life or the lives of others. Put on your boxing gloves and get ready to explore your anger to the very roots.

 ## HOW TO ASK FOR HELP AND HOW ANGER AFFECTS RELATIONSHIPS, FAMILY, AND HOME LIFE

Never Saying, "Don't Waste My Time."

Being short on time can make you short-tempered. I'm not saying that you're not appreciating your life. However, appreciating life doesn't mean that you must cram it full of accomplishments and "meaningful" activities just so you can proudly tell others about them. Instead, let somebody waste your time with something that they love. Allow a child to tell you at length about their truck or Lego sculpture, let your father drone on about his stamp collection, or sit and watch your aunt's pumpkins grow with her. Stop and allow your time to be wasted by something that brings you or others joy. Relax your shoulders. Allow a smile to creep across your lips.

My dad was always short on time from the day I was born. He was busy running his own business, supporting his family and investing energy in his hobbies. When he was diagnosed with end-stage cancer, he paradoxically slowed his life way down. He spent less time at work and more time at the local coffee shop, sipping his favorite brew and watching the passersby. At one of those coffee shop visits, he told me these small and seemingly insignificant moments were what really mattered in life. As I sip from the mug he bought from that coffee shop around that time, I have to agree. It's easy to lose sight of the important moments. Witness how many parents say that their kids grow up way too fast, and they really didn't appreciate the baby and toddler years as much as they should have.

Every time somebody annoys you, they're expressing some kind of hidden need. The idea of ill-expressed needs is most evident in small children. A toddler isn't getting enough attention according to him, so he throws crayons on the floor and stomps on them to see what his mom does. A preschooler is tired, and so she weeps endlessly at the difficulty of a simple card game. It turns out that, when we grow up, we aren't always much better than the small children we once were. Sometimes we're unable to express our needs clearly due to communication issues or being unsure of what our true needs are.

If somebody is driving you crazy, try to figure out what his or her underlying need might be. Then, try to communicate with the person by reflecting their needs in words. For example, "You feel unloved when I am feeling too sick to come over to your home, because you need connection with your loved ones. Does that sound about right?" Wait and see if you've properly assessed the need. If you have, then you can find some other way to fulfill the person's need if possible, or you can come to a consensus that it is not possible for you to meet the person's need right now. Either way, getting to the heart of the person's needs can shut down passive-aggressive or downright hostile interactions.

There's nothing like extreme grief and life upheaval to teach you who your real friends are and which family members care about you most of all. Of course, these are not easy lessons to learn, and one side effect can be some major trust issues. If you've had a friend disappear when you needed him or her most, you might feel very jaded about making new friends. What if any new person who shows up in your life turns out to be a fair-weather friend as well? What is the point of pouring out your heart to someone and becoming attached to him or her, only to find that they don't like the sick and scary looking version of you? Life is all about taking those sorts of risks in relationships. You can take some time for yourself, if you want, but remaining isolated in the long-term will not be good for your health.

You might also find yourself losing trust in some people that you want to keep, or must keep, in your life. Perhaps your mom didn't step up as much as you thought she would and bought gifts for herself instead of helping you out financially, or your sister flaked out on you and didn't come to a crucial family celebration during a time in your life when you thought it would be your last. In these circumstances, you've lost trust that can never be fully recovered in the same way. You can rebuild trust, but you'll have to adjust your expectations while you do so. Don't place your trust in that person, expecting that he or she will not disappoint you in the same way again. Instead, don't give the person another chance to disappoint you in the same way, but reach out to the person in a new way without losing hope entirely. If your mom didn't help you out financially, don't ask her for money again, but do ask her for babysitting or home-baked food if appropriate. If your sister refused to come to a family function, don't sign her up as your bridesmaid, but do call her on the phone for emotional support and exchange quirky gifts in the mail if appropriate. Give yourself time to grieve loss of trust, and then forge on forward bravely in new avenues of friendship and family bonding.

. . . .

Give yourself time to grieve loss of trust,
and then forge on forward bravely in new avenues
of friendship and family bonding.

. . . .

Eventually you will become the five people you hang around with most. At some point during our childhoods, we stop being raised primarily by our parents and begin to become more influenced by our peer groups. Though it is a sad fact to parents of kids who are growing into young adults, the people you spend your days with often shape the way you think about yourself and the world around you. No matter how positive a person may be, if he or she is in an abusive relationship or caught in a web of toxic friendships, that person will find themselves acting and reacting in accordance with the environmental pressures. Therefore, try to intentionally choose the company you keep, if possible, in your current situation.

If you're trapped at home with some less-than-helpful folks, invite people over who lift your spirit and bend your mind toward the positive. If you've been hanging out with friends who constantly leave you drained and in a bad mood, the very definition of psychic vampirism, cut those people off from your daily lived experience. And finally, if you don't have enough people spending time with you, be intentional about the influences that you draw into your life. Begin praying for the universe to draw people that you will want to emulate toward you. Ideally, you'll find people who are very much like you but who have progressed to a headspace or a place in life that you would like to occupy in a few years' time. Your friends can be your mentors and your life coaches. Visualize the sort of people you would like as friends and mentors in your life. Then pray for those people to enter your life.

You can't keep people in your life who want to leave it, and that can be very painful, especially if you are dealing with a divorce or illness that precipitated the ending of a friendship or other relationship. If this were a perfect world, the person who wanted to leave would announce clearly that he or she was doing so and assure you that there was nothing you could say or do to change his or her mind. Then, in this fantasy world, you would calmly agree with the person and go about your life without any further contact or drama.

Unfortunately, in this imperfect world, these two steps are often messed up. In my own life, instead of telling me clearly that the intention was to leave my life, people have resorted to other tactics. Severing contact unexpectedly, often called "ghosting," has happened to me with quite a few friends. Cruel behavior can also be a way that some people try to end a friendship or a relationship, with the intention being that you will be the one to end contact, and the person can be at peace, ironically feeling like he or she is not the bad guy since you're the one who severed contact. These tactics often backfire, in my case causing me to chase after the person to find out what's wrong and to see if I can do anything to mend fences. The drama caused by prolonging a severed connection with a friend or loved one can be painful, indeed. If you sense that somebody does not want to speak to you again, even if it seems like their reasoning is flawed, it is best to give them the gift of allowing them to move on.

Focus, instead, on deepening existing relationships in your life. The weirdest cultural phenomenon is that every day so many people ask how you are doing, and you are always supposed to respond with a positive or at least neutral answer. True friends will push a little deeper to find out how you really are. Family members may pry even further and ask the tougher questions: "How are you treating your wife and kids? How is work *really* going?" Depending on how private and introverted you tend to be, it can feel like an inquisition or a blessed relief when people ask you to tell them more about what is going on with you.

So what should you do if you're not being asked the deep questions you desire by people with whom you want to bond? I can tell you what not to do from my experience. Whenever I tried to fish for sympathy or to give too much information to somebody who was not ready, I came off as an attention hog. This made such people less likely to listen deeply and to engage with me in sharing what was going on in their own lives. Instead, first find a confidant to whom you can tell everything, even if that person is a therapist or your own journal for now. Second, begin asking some of your friends and family your own tough questions about how they're really doing in life. Initiating the self-disclosure by asking them to share can help people open up and realize that you are trying to get closer to them. Ask a loved one how he or she is doing, and follow up to find out what's really going on in their lives and reconnect.

Anger as a Form of Fear

If you find yourself sitting with anger toward someone, try to get at the heart of the fears that might be feeding your anger. After all, anger can be a tool to allow yourself not to be stepped upon. Lawyers are often loathed because they happen to be there as a target for anger when somebody is going through a tough spot in life, whether it be family, civil, or criminal law dealings. Similarly, a doctor or even a car mechanic might be the target of ire when really the circumstances are to blame. Wherever there is anger, there is often the underlying emotion of fear. For example, jealousy is expressed angrily, but at its heart, jealousy is the fear of losing something or someone you love.

Ask yourself: Why did I make this person a target for all my anger? You may be afraid or adrift in a sea of uncertainty. Chances are, there are many unfair things that are happening to you right now. You might have been struck by illness through no fault of your own, or you may be struggling with unfair interpersonal issues or financial burdens.

Trauma is when a person's faith in the general goodness of the world is shaken. By this definition, you might be the very picture of trauma. Wrestling with the big questions of life can be the greatest blessing and greatest curse of a major life transition. Allow yourself to go on an inward journey while lashing outward as little as possible, though people may make themselves easy targets for retaliation.

Anger Is Your Soul Crying Out for Boundaries

You already know that fear can be the root of angry feelings. It's also true that anger can be the direct result of a lack of necessary boundaries. If you find yourself lashing out at somebody, that angry exchange could have potentially been avoided by setting up some healthy boundaries and sticking to them.

You may get irritated with people helping you out too much, talking about too many personal topics, talking about you behind your back, or visiting your home unannounced. If you find yourself angry with them, consider setting some boundaries. It may reduce your anger or eliminate it entirely. My stepdad says that fish and houseguests start to smell a bit after three days. He's right. Plenty of bickering occurred within my family when my parents had to come and help me take care of my kids during chemotherapy. Tension grew. The food supply ran out when no one thought to bring more for the extra mouths to feed. House rules were ignored. Misunderstandings arose. It was just a general grumpy nightmare having several overworked volunteers in the household caring for me.

· ·

People don't have to understand everything about your situation, and you don't owe them your entire life story, but giving people permission not to understand anything more than the fact that you're having a hard time doesn't have to be a chore.

· ·

Here's a phrase that you can use any time somebody is getting on your raw nerves by coming a little too close to a tender subject. Say, "You might not understand, and I hope you never have to." People don't have to understand everything about your situation, and you don't owe them your entire life story, but giving people permission not to understand anything more than the fact that you're having a hard time doesn't have to be a chore.

It can be entirely frustrating or rage-inducing when people question your choices after your choices have been limited by circumstances beyond your control. If you decide not to choose a solution because the benefits are not worth the personal or financial costs, you may receive pushback from people who don't think you're doing everything you can or that you have thought through things completely.

Know that when people seem to not be on the same page as you, the confusion may have nothing to do with the issue itself, but about the projection of their own fears. Remember that it isn't your job to make people understand your life, and you are under no obligation to explain your choices to anyone. Gently change the subject or firmly tell somebody if they are getting near your boundaries. Say something like, "Excuse me, I know that you're just trying to help, but I really have this situation under control as much as I am able to in these circumstances. Could we please talk about something else?"

My dad was the sort of man who really knew how to start and end an argument. If there was somebody who was breaking my heart, whether it was with a bad chemistry grade or an interpersonal problem, he was ready to go find that person and make him or her sorry. The problem with such a personality type arises when there is a problem that can't be solved with aggression. If I was sad and disappointed in myself, my frustrated father would simply come down on me harder, making me feel worse and hardly solving the problem.

You, yourself, may be a similar sort of problem-solver. If not, you will undoubtedly have some friends or relatives who seem to be inexplicably angry with you over whatever life challenges are thrown your way. If you are the target of anger from somebody who has no reason to be angry with you, have compassion, but be sure to set some limits so that he or she doesn't walk all over you in the name of knowing what is best for you. If you are the type who typically can solve any problem through confronting it angrily and head-on, be aware of who is likely to become the target of your ire.

Be assertive instead of aggressive. Children can learn how to be assertive by comparing assertiveness to aggression and passiveness. Through books and stories, my children discovered that being aggressive can come off as being like a monster, roaring what you want and intimidating others to achieve your goals. Being passive can be more like being a mouse, using a tiny or whiny voice to articulate your needs. Neither one of these, they learned, is very effective on their mother, so I encourage them to be themselves, neither mice nor monsters. Of course, your own way of doing things may not tend to be assertive. In order to be the best advocate for yourself that you can be, it's time to polish up your assertiveness skills.

Be direct, be clear, and be insistent. At this stage in my healing, I still find myself dancing around what I want. For example, when I want reassurance, I might start fishing for compliments by being self-effacing when I should just come out and ask for some reassuring words. Are there any times when you roar like a monster or whine like a mouse? Think about what you really want to see and hear from the people around you and ask for those things directly.

Comparison Is a Thief of Joy

We all know that comparing one's success to that of another can be counterproductive. The endless treadmill of keeping up with the Joneses is a silly one if you're constantly trying to one-up your neighbor by buying a better car or electronic gadget. It's easy for a spiritual person to pat himself or herself on the back for not getting caught up in competing for material gain. However, something insidious and strange happens when tragedy and misfortune befall even the most kind-hearted and mindful person. If you formerly enjoyed life circumstances that have evaporated due to trauma, you may find yourself dismayed when the lives of your friends and family keep progressing and moving on, seemingly leaving you behind in the dust and ruins of your former life.

After my friend Sarah's life was in upheaval due to her second husband's ongoing custody battle with his ex-wife, Sarah found it impossible to follow along with the lives of successful people. The joy of others either seemed unobtainable to herself or reminded her painfully of her failed first marriage. Their lives seemed entirely detached from her life. But in time she gained perspective. I am happy to say that other peoples' bounty now reminds her that wonderful things can happen. Make a list of people in your life who are successful role models for you. If you can't name enough, pray for spirit to draw into your life five people who can uplift your life.

Keep Your Kindness When You're Angry

Our language demonizes anger as an emotion. For women especially, anger is seen as something that is off-putting at best. For men, anger is seen as something scary and dangerous. In children, anger is quashed immediately. Children are asked to go to time-out and are isolated when they display anger, without much real instruction on how to make use of anger in life as a motivator.

When my daughter was told that kindness is a superpower, she scoffed at this idea and told me that anybody can be kind. "Yes," I agreed, "But not just anyone can be kind all the time. That would be a superpower." I strive constantly toward superpower-level kindness, and I'm not always successful. I can be just as bitter and defensive as anyone else, but if I am, I've let the person who has offended me take something precious from me: my kindness. While you're convalescing, treat your kindness as if it were a wounded bird that you are nursing back to health. Keep your kindness safe, keep it away from predators, and by all means don't let it fly out the window.

· ·

While you're convalescing, treat your kindness
as if it were a wounded bird that you are nursing
back to health. Keep your kindness safe, keep it
away from predators, and by all means don't
let it fly out the window.

· ·

If you're feeling angry, take steps toward making things better right now. For example, if you are angry at someone else's attitude, take the time to write a letter, regardless whether it will ever be sent, after you've had some time to vent and cool down. If you're angry at how your illness or trauma has shaped your life, become an activist and share information or work to make change by raising money or gathering signatures for a petition.

Feeling angry isn't nearly as unpleasant as feeling both impotent and angry, so use your anger toward a productive goal. You can use it to heave yourself out of bed for the day, make some phone calls to a lawyer to make sure that your best interests are being served, or throw away all your cigarettes and quit smoking for good. Don't ignore your anger—harness it. Once you give yourself a constructive outlet, you'll find that you don't have as much negative fallout from your rage. Besides, being angry protects you from being walked all over by those who otherwise might mistakenly take your exhaustion or lack of motivation for weakness.

Exercise: Creating Angry Art–Slam Poetry

There are numerous ways to be angry with art, and I only wish that I had a kiln so that I could push and punch some clay around. As it is, writing is often my weapon of choice, and slam poetry is a well-known way to arrange angry words.

Poetry doesn't have to rhyme, and it doesn't have to be something beautiful that someone would want to cross-stitch and hang up on the wall. In fact, some of the best poetry uses everyday language that isn't flowery at all. Your poems can even have curse words. You don't need to share your poems with anyone at all. Try starting with an angry phrase, repeating it, and experimenting to find some sort of rhythm.

If you want, you can share your poetry with your closest friends, or you can write everything in a journal. Try keeping a scrapbook during your treatment or healing journey and fill it with artifacts that remind you of the experience. When you are done with your journey, don't keep the scrapbook. The process of writing the poetry and keeping the books together can be therapy in and of itself, and there is no need to revisit some of the hard times you have experienced once you are through if you don't want to. In my own scrapbook, I don't regret any of the things that I wrote out in private, even when they were angry and emotional things. Putting my feelings down on paper allowed me to feel like I could move on, rather than stew angrily ad infinitum.

HOW ANGER AFFECTS WORK LIFE, PLANNING, AND LOGISTICS

Make Room for Calm

Do you have time to meditate every day? If the idea of adding some meditation to your day feels like a chore, then you probably have too much going on in your life right now. Simplify things. Make some room in your life to welcome calm moments and peaceful thoughts. If you must schedule time on your calendar for calm, do so. A seated meditation in the garden, a peaceful bubble bath, or playing around with a musical instrument or hobby might be just what the doctor ordered to reduce the massive level of stress in your life right now. If you don't make room for calm moments, they will never come on their own. There will never be a point in your life when you say, "Gee, nothing is going on. I guess now is the best time to relax!" You've got to invest in those times for yourself. Add some calm moments to your calendar and make a plan for a stress-busting activity, such as meditation or a bubble bath.

Busy people always feel at their happiest when they're burning the candle at both ends. A mom friend of mine is currently at a high point in her life. Monica has both her kids in several extracurricular activities and has big personal projects on the horizon. She's volunteering for two different organizations and leading an academic association. She feels joyful, albeit overwhelmed. In contrast, when she was recovering from a back injury, she had to simplify her life to one or two activities a day. She became overwhelmed and dissatisfied with life. If her only task for the day was to go to the bank, she felt an even greater sense of inertia than when she had to squeeze grocery shopping in between a dentist appointment and her kid's sport practice. She had begun to use busy activity as a crutch to avoid thinking about her feelings.

Near the end of my treatment I had the pleasure of going on a retreat with other young cancer survivors. We learned rock climbing, which quickly became a metaphor for life. I was surprised to find that even people who were much sicker than I were able to climb seemingly sheer rock walls in the mountains. Rock climbing was harder for me than I anticipated, though. While at my peak health, I would have been able to forcibly monkey my way up those rocks through sheer strength of muscle. In my weakened condition, I found that I had to rely on strategy and my developing skills.

One tip given to me by a seasoned climber was basically this: move from position of rest to position of rest, rather than position of stress to position of stress. By this he meant that you shouldn't use a burst of strength to land yourself on a precarious rock outcropping, groping with shaky hands desperately for something that will support your weight. Instead, carefully pick your way up the rock wall, trying each new toehold two or three times before taking a step upward and surveying a new area to decide your next move. By using this strategy, my rock climbs became no more difficult than climbing a set of stairs, even though I couldn't even manage a chin-up with my atrophied arm muscles. The metaphor here is that life can sometimes be like a challenging rock climb. You don't necessarily know what difficulties feel like in the future, so it behooves you not to run out your strength hoping that you will be adequately supported when the time comes.

Exercise: Physical Release of Anger

Consider how you find outlets for angry feelings. Is there a sport or other activity that makes you feel relaxed and tired afterward? Even if you can't afford to do such activities right now or you are not healthy enough to do them, can you re-create the feeling of being happily tired out from a day of activity now that your activities might be limited? The only good news about being sick was that I could get pleasantly tired from the smallest activities. I felt like I was running a marathon when I was just packing my kids' school lunches, and I'd have to take breaks along the way. But, even if I was tired by everyday activities, they weren't cathartic. I had to find other ways to get physical, like flicking paint onto a piece of paper to make angry splotches that matched my feelings.

When my mom was a child, she would scream into a pillow when she was angry. When I was a child, I took things a little further and punched my pillow whenever

I was mad. Pillows are excellent recipients of anger. You can also squeeze a stress ball or rub your thumb in the indentation of a worry stone. You can make your own stress ball out of a balloon filled with flour. When I'm feeling well, martial arts, running, and weightlifting are all cathartic ways for me to release my anger in a physical way. When I'm not feeling well, I tend to have more pent-up rage inside due to the lack of a physical outlet.

SELF-CARE AND SPIRITUALITY

Be Gentle with Yourself and Don't Beat Yourself Up

You don't have to stop trying, and you don't have to feel bad for not being just like your former self. Release yourself from the idea of comparing your present self to whatever you were like during the past. Yes, this is easier said than done, and it will require some grieving in the process. Instead, shift your focus to the things that you are doing well in life, even if they are small. It's okay to ask for reassurance from loved ones if you do so directly and don't confuse them by fishing for compliments. Remember to also reach for love and acceptance deep within yourself. Ultimately, external validation will never make up for self-abuse if you have consistent negative self-talk.

There's probably no going back to the way life used to be. Your home may have changed, as well as your interpersonal relationships and workflow. Perhaps you're now on disability payments for the first time or trying to learn to use mobility equipment. Your life has been forever changed, and the first way you'll cope is to come to terms with one chapter of your life ending and another one just beginning.

. . . .

Your life has been forever changed, and the first way you'll cope is to come to terms with one chapter of your life ending and another one just beginning.

. . . .

Grief for your old life may be so strong and confusing that you start missing the things that you hate. If you've lost a job, that ordinary and boring daily work might be viewed with wistful nostalgia. If there's any way that you can say goodbye with proper closure, please do so. A retirement party might be appropriate. When I discovered I had kidney disease, I threw a party, and I threw a going-away party for my breasts before my double mastectomies. I'll be starting a medication that has a contraindication with grapefruit, so I might just throw myself a grapefruit party before I get started. A party may not be your style. You might be the type to want to write a goodbye letter to some aspect of your old life or to burn a symbol of what you are losing. Give yourself the gift of closure.

It Doesn't All Rely on You
If you're ready to release all of your troubles to the Divine, by all means affirm to yourself, "I am powerless over this problem that I didn't cause and I cannot fix, so I turn all of my problem over to spirit." If you're not ready to take such a drastic step as giving over all your power to even a higher power, take a baby step toward that relief. It is only within the last couple of years that I have been able to admit to myself that everything doesn't

rely on me. Yes, I used to at least subconsciously think that every outcome was my responsibility. I felt fully responsible for the happiness and sadness of my loved ones, for their failures as well as their potential future triumphs. It is too great a burden to bear, so right now I can freely admit that I'm not the most important contributor to every life project.

As a control freak, Dave wanted to be completely in charge of his own destiny at all times. As a codependent, he wanted to take care of everyone that he loved and take responsibility for all their faults and failings. In situations where he felt powerless, he couldn't feel relaxed and able to turn his attention away from the problem at hand. Instead, he felt increasingly desperate, like a rodent scrabbling to escape a bucket. He couldn't let go. We're all coming to spiritual principles as equals, but from different cultural directions, so some people may find it easier to "let go and let God" than Dave did. Whenever possible, I like to take power into my own hands and manifest change. However, I need to acknowledge that sometimes change isn't all up to me.

If you're feeling a loss of control, try to find the little things in life that you can control without making yourself into a pain for everyone else around you. Hopefully, small choices like what you wear in the morning can bring you some sense of pride in your life choices. Don't be afraid to admit to someone who feels clueless about why you're so adamant about some life choices that part of your reasoning includes the lack of control you feel in other aspects of your life. Recognize when you're grasping for control in life and do so in appropriately small chunks.

Why do we feel entitled to control a life that isn't fair? Nobody wants to believe that they are an entitled brat, though we all can recognize them: the man who screams impotently at a waitress because he can't be served breakfast late in the day, or the woman who is abusive to her grandchildren and then shocked when her daughter no longer brings them over to visit. In reality, we all believe that we are entitled to certain rights, and our politics and laws are structured around those entitlements. Where is the line? It's a moving target based in part on your culture as well as your age, stage in life, and personal experiences. For example, you may or may not believe that you are entitled to health care or help from able-bodied folk when you are ill.

Entitlement can cause anger when your expectations are not met, causing you to rage against the injustice of it all. Even if I don't like to think about myself as entitled, I surprise myself with feelings of entitlement. I realize now that I am not entitled to the friendship and kindness of others simply because I am friendly and kind to them. When I relax expectations, I am free to treat people with loving kindness without requiring anything in return, and I am equally free to refuse to be treated improperly without trying to force others to be something they're not.

Anger at God

In some faith traditions, being angry at one's god may seem odd or inappropriate. However, I maintain that spirit is big enough to take all the anger that one person or even many people may throw at it. All day long, in the modern media as well as in classic mythology, we hear stories of gods being defended to the death by their followers but, in reality, divine beings need no defense. They are mighty. Perhaps God, more than any other therapist or best friend, deserves to hear your fury.

If you're new to prayer or feeling a little rusty, you don't have to worry too much about formatting your talk with the Divine. After all, if you're angry, you're probably not up for the flowery language and poetic epithets of traditionally written prayers. Instead, call upon your own words as if spirit were a close friend and confidant. Express your rage and shout your questions. After one such session of tearful prayer, I received an answer that gave me peace. I was crying to the Goddess about why she seemed to support my marriage, I guess by not striking me down with lightning on my wedding day, to one who would leave me when I was feeling sick, beaten down, and mutilated from treatment. In a dream, my Goddess came to me and told me that I had not left the path that she had ordained for me. I felt isolated and damaged from my cancer experience, but she told me that my hands were still open to help others and hold companionship. That my heart was still open and there were many who held me in theirs. That my spirit was still mine to share, and there were many who walked with me in spirit. My anger was placated by my symbolic dream talking with my deity of choice, and I hope that expressing your rage at your own source of divinity will be equally healing. Express your anger at spirit, if any, and seek a lesson in return.

Do you see more evil in the world these days? You may meet some downright ghoulish people when you reach the lowest points in your life. There may be the cold and clinical doctor who tells you that there's no hope, such as when I was told that my mental illness would leave me institutionalized. You might have people carelessly ask you if they can have your belongings after you divorce, as if all they care about are material things. These sorts of behaviors can be a terrible blow to the heart. Not only can they leave you feeling like a burden to those who are actually happy to have you in their lives, but they often create more trust issues to work through and serious doubts about the goodness of the world and people in general.

• •

Whether or not true evil exists, it is counterproductive to try to sort and categorize people in your life based on such a worldview, and it can be detrimental to dwell on evil stories and fears.

• •

It's certainly up to your own theology whether you believe in mustache-twirling evil people or whether you think that there are just right and wrong actions and that people are just messy shades of gray. I've found that even the sweetest people I know have done nasty things to others in their past. Whether or not true evil exists, it is counterproductive to try to sort and categorize people in your life based on such a worldview, and it can be detrimental to dwell on evil stories and fears. Instead, seek out the good things in the world. Quiz the good people you know to find out what they have in common, and what traits you can nourish in yourself. Bring out the good in yourself and others, and don't dwell on anything truly awful that somebody has done to you.

Exercise: Letting Go of Anger Completely

This is an exercise to let go of anger completely. Keep in mind that today is not going to mark the end of the experience of anger in your life. The average person experiences anger several times a week, and to do otherwise would be abnormal. The exercise of releasing anger is meant to be one repeated as often as necessary.

For this exercise, you'll need a bowl of water and a healthy plant that you intend to water. Sit in meditation and allow yourself to think of something that angers you. Fully allow yourself to experience anger. You needn't let yourself go through the machinations of imagining retaliation against a person, but instead focus on how the anger feels in your body as it washes over you. Feel any areas of your body that feel tight, tense, shaky, hot, or energized. In your mind's eye, see the energy of your anger flow to your hands as you ball them into fists. When all the angry energy is in your two fists, dip them in the bowl of water and spread your fingers, forcing the anger energy into the bowl of water. Allow any of those physical sensations of anger to drain from your body as you take notice of and relax the parts of your body that you observed holding your anger. When you are done, pour the water onto the plant, knowing that Mother Nature will allow your energy to be harmlessly transformed into life-giving energy for the plant. Release and transform your anger, then observe how it feels to let go of the anger that you felt. Repeat this exercise on multiple days if necessary.

Chapter 3

J

BARGAINING WHEN THINGS GO SIDEWAYS

Doctors and judges must hear it all. When bad news is delivered, people will go to great lengths to try to get the authority figure to say something else. Some people might try to bribe them with gifts or threaten the professional with formal disciplinary action. Most people will do absolutely anything to stay alive, healthy, and financially secure. When nothing can be done about a potentially life-changing problem, there can be a certain level of emotional bargaining that goes on internally or outwardly. You can use your natural impulses to bargain or argue in a positive way. Bargain with yourself about healthy lifestyle changes, getting what you deserve in your career search, or finally deciding how you deserve to be treated.

A Buddhist belief is that everything in life is impermanent. The idea of impermanence can be frightening. Of course, things will change. Adorable babies grow up into headstrong adults that move away to start lives of their own. We, too, grow old and die. Our bodies eventually rot away, even if embalmed, and even the toughest grave markers suffer the wear and tear of Mother Nature.

. . . .

Change is always happening in the world, and
embracing change as a spiritual expression of
the Divine can be freeing.

. . . .

As we all march inexorably forward in life toward the end of this lifetime, many work hard to make an indelible mark on the world. But what if one decides to go the opposite route and leave as soft a footprint on the earth as possible? Change is always happening in the world, and embracing change as a spiritual expression of the Divine can be freeing. No matter what you do in order to cling to a season of your life, that season will change in some way. You can hedge your bets with back-up plans and redundancy, but there's nothing you can do to guarantee that you will leave behind any legacy in which you have placed your hopes. Embrace the greater guarantee of change by meditating on life's impermanence. Visualize the seasons changing or the moon's cycles. Find comfort in the fact that the pattern is that there is always change, and so change must await everyone and everything.

At some point, you're going to hit a low point in your life and, when you're going through a crisis of faith, that low point may come quicker or seem much lower. My stepdad quit being a minister after his wife and daughter died in the same year.

Serious maladies and facing death can cause us to wonder why bad things happen to good people. Losing faith can be a painful process. The happiest patients are those who were either comfortable in their faith or had no faith at all. Patients who struggle with their faith tend to have poor health outcomes since losing faith can also cause feelings of shame and fear that can complicate an already rough time.

If you're suffering a crisis of faith, first realize that a crisis of faith is okay. You don't have to be steadily pious your entire life, and indeed a crisis can strengthen faith even if you don't force it. Relax about your spiritual seeking and imagine yourself as a wise person heading up into the mountains or wandering the woods to seek the answers of life. You can even drop some spiritual activities if they bring you more anger than solace during this time. I had to stop attending some faith discussion groups that raised my hackles until I could be in a better place to receive the message. Doubt is a good thing. It will allow you to either come back to your faith stronger than ever or find something even better.

HOW TO ASK FOR HELP AND HOW BARGAINING AFFECTS RELATIONSHIPS, FAMILY, AND HOME LIFE

An Arrow to the Heart

When a loved one wounds us, we often ask ourselves why the wound occurred. An inevitable spiral of blame, self-flagellation, and hand-wringing about how to right the wrong that has happened can be counterproductive to healing. Imagine the case of being wounded by an arrow in the woods. The first reaction should not be to demand who shot the arrow and begin finding fault. Instead, the first reaction to being wounded should be to find safe refuge and tend to the wound. Indeed, please pull out the arrow before finding the shooter.

If you feel betrayed by or disappointed in a loved one, the first reaction may be to confront that person and to bare your soul. For a vulnerable person such as yourself, confrontation can end up rolling together conflicting and confused emotions, spreading and deepening the hurt. Instead, tend to your own emotions before opening the lines of communication with a person who may have hurt you, intentionally or unintentionally. Think of a situation in which somebody else has hurt you and you still feel the pain. Take a moment to self-soothe, whether through prayer and meditation, or perhaps simply seeking out something that makes you smile. Allow yourself to recover emotionally before reaching out for understanding from the offender.

Self-care is a struggle for the caretaker type of person. I am sure that many of you are nodding in agreement if you find yourself more likely to tell another person to eat a healthy meal or wear a warm coat than to look after those basic essentials for yourself. Before I learned the basics of self-care, I was terrified that any such focus would turn me into a selfish monster. I was comforted when my therapist told me that it would be nearly impossible for me to turn selfish simply by being kind to myself.

Think of self-care as driving on a road between two extreme ditches. On the right hand of the road is the ditch of selfishness. On the left hand of the road is the ditch of willful self-negligence and self-destruction. Where do you normally drive on this road? Is there any way that you can drive a little closer to the center than you normally do? Can you allow yourself to drive a little closer to the shoulder of self-care since you are sick right now?

When ignoring my own self-care, I attended my mom's spiritual study group while already in a bad frame of mind. I was still recovering from treatment, getting monthly maintenance medications in the chemo ward even as the radiation burns faded from my body and thick tufts of hair had grown back to cover my head. I was going through a brutal divorce, experiencing cruelty and disloyalty so shocking that I couldn't believe it was happening even as I watched the schism build before my eyes. The topic of the spiritual study group I was attending was unity.

As the friendly group of spiritual scholars and seekers warmly discussed eschewing adversarial thinking, I became angrier and angrier. In the past year I had already seen friends and family attack each other and drive each other apart with betrayals. In that moment, the idea of turning the other cheek was abhorrent to me. I almost got right up to walk out of the room, but I steeled myself instead. I forced myself to ask curious questions to see how these people, many of whom were older than me and thus presumably had suffered situations like mine, could possibly seek unity above all else. Apparently, unity, unlike love, is not blind. If you have somebody with whom you want to make peace during this time of your life, realize that it may be impossible or simply not your obligation, and that self-care can often mean putting yourself first.

A friend of mine we'll call Tanya was unable to ever find unity with her father because of his traumatic treatment of her during childhood. Tanya was trafficked for sex work starting from a young age. As an adult, she was diagnosed with dissociative identity disorder and lost custody of her daughters. Since there was no chance of getting a resolution or apology from her father, and she wasn't even allowed to write a letter to her kids, Tanya had to focus on her own inner work in order to meet the requirements to earn back the rights to see her children. Happily, she has come a long way and is now able to be the mother that her kids need. If she had stayed in a place of blame and anger, she might never have been able to reach this peaceful resolution.

As Long as You Have Good Intentions, You Win Any Conflict
Nobody is immune from being painted as the bad guy in social situations. Though the mantle of victimhood may be comforting and a great defense at times, it is not a perfect solution. Even if you really do feel unable to carry out your responsibilities, those whose expectations you do not meet will not necessarily show perfect compassion. You won't be able to please everyone, even if you try your very hardest. You'll still receive criticism on your life choices.

. . . .

You don't have to beat yourself up if you have
tried at something and failed. Simply set the
intention to be better and move forward.

. . . .

Take a new outlook on being a good person for this time in your life and decide that if you can live with your own choices, those choices are the right choices for you. If you don't measure your own actions by their intentions, you'll have no meaningful guideposts for the present moment in time. You don't have to beat yourself up if you have tried at something and failed.

Simply set the intention to be better and move forward. Likewise, if somebody's expectations for you are way off base, you don't have to spend too much time and energy trying to live up to those expectations. Instead, decide what good intentions you have for yourself and the world around you. If people around you are cruel to you about your choices, remember that they are the ones who have to sleep at night after behaving in the way they have. You only need to worry about your own heart and soul. If you are a good person, you can relax. Set some good intentions in your mind and let nobody stop you or turn you aside from those goals and thoughts.

Meditation: Searching for Justice in the Universe

Meditate for a moment on the concept of justice. Though individual instances of what constitutes justice may change over time and across cultures, all human societies have some definition of justice. What do you picture when you think about justice? Do you imagine a superhero or some other character meting out justice, do you imagine yourself being just, or do you picture justice as a natural tipping of the scales that the universe carries out all by itself?

In the Western concept of karma, the spiritual scales of good and evil are balanced out over time. Thus, if someone does bad things in the world, that negativity will return to him or her in this lifetime or the next. You might wonder what sort of thing you did to "deserve" what happened to you, or you might even find yourself secretly wishing somebody nastier than you were suffering your misfortune instead. The anger you are feeling is okay, but any sense of shame should be stamped out. You have done nothing to deserve any amount of suffering that you are experiencing from natural illness or a personal trauma. The spiritual concept of karma can act as a comfort for you that those who are behaving badly will receive their own comeuppance even if you are not privy to what happens to them. Relax and allow the universe to roll out its own form of justice. All you can do in your lifetime is act with integrity. Visualize the concept of justice. What does it look like to you? In your mind's eye, see all things right with you in the world.

HOW BARGAINING AFFECTS WORK LIFE, PLANNING, AND LOGISTICS

Just for Today

A common recovery slogan is that one should take things one day at a time. It means that even if yesterday you were feeling yourself at your worst, today is a new day. Having a perspective that focuses on the present day will also stop you from borrowing trouble from your future by thinking about how bad things might become. When I was at my most ill, I had to break down my time even further to living life five minutes at a time.

Recognize your good moments or days. Notice how long they may be. From a spiritual frame of mind, a single instant can stretch into an eternity, so don't be sad if you only have fleeting moments of refuge from pain or suffering. Wait until you land on one of those moments or days or weeks and allow yourself to stretch it out by fully immersing yourself in the present. Tell yourself that, just for today, you're going to put off dreading the future or re-living the past. Wait until you are having a good moment today and find a way to linger in that moment. Put off anything that you can delay so that you can stay in your moment of peace.

Don't try to solve all your problems at once. Some people are procrastinators, and some people are such a polar opposite that they become overwhelmed easily by too many commitments. When one becomes indisposed by life circumstances, these personality traits can feel like a barrier to wellness. If you have a long treatment plan or court case, it can be easy to start living months in the future and end up planning too much for yourself. Conversely, you might find yourself having trouble giving up activities or duties that were yours when life was normal.

Take some time to write down in your journal some of the pressing issues that you need to prioritize. You don't have to make a timeline if you have many unknown components to your problems. The exercise is to simply give voice to some of them. I know that you might be worried that they might get worse if you're focusing on these problems. Understand that the purpose of this exercise is to prioritize them so that you can strike them down one by one. Don't forget to identify the "problems" that really are wishes and needs. Pick one that is a priority and take one small action toward fulfilling that need today. Delegate problem-solving to others whenever possible.

If I Can Worry and Strategize at 3 a.m., I Can Do So When It Happens

Postponing feelings really works. In fact, if you allow yourself some time to self-soothe and relax, you'll be able to come back to problem-solving with renewed clarity. Consider this the next time that you are having an argument with somebody that you love. Take a break from the argument that lasts about twenty minutes. Any shorter and you'll still be angry. Any longer and you'll just be avoiding the problem, allowing it to spiral into something bigger than it needs to be. During your break from the argument, focus on soothing yourself, rather than replaying or rehearsing the argument.

Similarly, if you find yourself catastrophizing in the wee hours of the morning instead of sleeping, allow yourself to sleep on it. If the thoughts keep returning, allow them to float through you to be remembered another day. If you're worrying about your own death, there's no chance that you'll forget your mortality overnight, but if there is some detail you need to re-member, go ahead and write it down.

There are no ends to the negative "what-if" scenarios that you can dream up about the progression of your misfortune or the reactions of people in your life to what you're enduring. If you've only got two or three worst-case scenarios, you might just not yet have given yourself enough time to think of more. One of my doctors interrupted me as I offloaded my specula-tions and said, "Yeah, yeah, well, we can drown in what-ifs all day long, but that's not going to help anything." At some point, it's important to move forward with your life decisions and then forgive yourself afterward if things go sideways. Assure yourself that you've made the best decisions that you could with the in-formation that you had at the time.

One thing that can help when you're catastrophizing is to tell another person or to write down your worries. Sometimes, putting words to the worries helps one realize just how silly and unlikely they are. If you are brave enough to share with another person, the two of you can laugh about it. Sometimes, I'm only brave enough to share silly worries with my gods, and I feel like we can laugh about them together too. Make a list of some of your worst-case scenario worries. Be as detailed as you can. Write in complete sentences when documenting your worries. You might find that some of your fears evaporate under scrutiny.

If You Get Bored, You're Not Truly Giving Space

Larry was an active friend of mine who booked out his weekends three months in advance with hiking trails, travel, and continuing education. When he lost his license to practice counseling due to an error he made with his continuing education requirements, he was forced to take two low-paying jobs that required him to work long hours. As a security guard, he spent his time glumly watching closed-circuit camera feeds while suppressing his regrets about not doing anything more "useful" with his career.

Over time, he realized that he was not allowing himself the time that he needed to process his feelings. Any time that he was not working, he was frantically trying to distract himself from his emotions through housework and playing video games. That meant that the second he lay down in bed to sleep, his brain was finally free to think of all the terrible thoughts he had avoided throughout the day. I'm not saying that playing video games is a bad use of anyone's time, but for Larry it became a band-aid for a wound that desperately needed oxygen. He eventually made the decision to meditate at breakfast and confront some of the emotions he knew he couldn't avoid. Take note of how you spend your time if you are bored. Find what activities you can reduce or eliminate to add time for meditation or interpersonal connection.

Exercise: The Goal Game

Gamification is a modern word that refers to taking something from ordinary life and making it into a game so that you can feel motivated to reach a goal. Even as an adult, you can gamify your own life so that you feel that you're saving the world in the same way you did in your imagination as a child. You would actually be saving your own world.

A simple way to create a game is to set up a reward system for a fitness goal. For example, a friend of mine was bedbound due to a motorcycle injury that smashed her pelvis. She set a goal to be able to sit up in a wheelchair. After some time, she set her sights on arguing with her insurance company to receive physical therapy. After years of work and progressing little by little, she can now stand and walk for short periods of time. Set up some goals in your life and a reward for yourself along the way. Try to make a game out of earning points toward your own recovery.

Exercise: Making "Yes" and "No" Stones

Do you think in extremes? Do you think that you need to work full-time or not at all? Do you think that your life will not be complete if you go through a radical surgery such as an amputation? Do you feel like your relationship needs to progress to the next level or your life will not be properly lived? You might just be one of those people who thinks in terms of black and white. Extreme thinking isn't necessarily bad, because it offers clarity. Consider the simple action of making "yes" or "no" stones. Find a black stone meaning "no" and a white stone meaning "yes" and place them in a bag. Hold and shake the bag while concentrating on a question and using your intuition. Then draw a stone.

So many big questions can be answered in extremes, but you'll notice that if you use your "yes" and "no" stones for everything, you'll start getting conflicting answers once you get into the details of your life plans. It turns out that everything in life falls into a sort of gray area in between. If your stones show you a conflict, that is where you need to make a compromise. Make a set of "yes" and "no" stones in order to get all-or-nothing thinking out of your system and to explore its limitations.

SELF-CARE AND SPIRITUALITY

Self-Empowerment

Spirituality is empowering. You know that you are in control of you own destiny and that you have the power to create change and manifestation around you from within. However, it can be easy to take your own personal responsibility a bit too far and feel like you're failing the world if you're not making a big and immediate impact. The professors in my doctoral degree program kept telling us, "Finish your dissertation first, then go save the world." This was in response to those students who picked an overly ambitious topic for their dissertation proposal. Letting go of some of your most grandiose plans, at least temporarily, can be a difficult part of self-care.

Remember that we all depend on others to create the world we want to see. We stand on the shoulders of multiple thousands of ancestors who made us what we are today. Each of us are powerful individuals who are but one link in a chain. One way to gain perspective of how your power fits into the grand scheme of things is to research your ancestry and name some of your ancestors while learning what you can about them. Recognize that you are the product of the love of countless generations.

. . . .

Recognize that you are the product of the love
of countless generations.

. . . .

Looking into the future, beyond your lifetime, is a stage that everyone goes through near the end of life as they evaluate what contributions they've made to the world. If you have a potentially life-limiting illness, or even if you do not, you may find that the next generation of humanity brings you hope and comfort. If you have young children of your own, you may find that writing them letters to be opened on each birthday until adulthood brings you comfort. If you don't have biological children, you can still choose to impart your wisdom and have just as much impact on the next generation.

Reaching out as an aunt or uncle can connect you with the community and with humanity as a whole. In the Hindu spiritual dance community, older women are called *akka*, or "auntie." Those akkas feel comfortable offering a hug or even a light scolding to children, related or not, who scamper throughout the temple where they dance. As a person going through adversity, you have much to offer the younger generation and might receive a warm welcome if you reach out to elementary schools as a guest speaker.

How Lucky You Are to Be in Limbo

Western secular culture has no patience for spiritual strife. If there is a death in the family, we are expected to get over it after a few days off work. There are no rites of passage for boys becoming men and girls becoming women. There is little sympathy when a pet dies or a marriage dissolves and no sympathy at all for an addiction, breakup of a long-term relationship, onset of mental illness, or loss of one's faith. Major life transitions and emotional upheavals were once believed to be spiritual afflictions, and many cultures honor the time when one must wander to seek his or her fortune or retreat to restore his or her understanding of the world. What if instead of saying, "It already happened, so snap out of it," your friends and family said, "How lucky you are to be on this spiritual journey! Take as long as you need to, and we will offer you whatever aid we can but wish you well on your way"? Reframe your current journey toward wellness as a spiritual seeking.

A platitude often offered to those in emotional distress is that every cloud has a silver lining. It can be terrible, in times of great grief, to try to notice the blessings or lessons hidden among the tragedies. Certainly, if you are not ready to seek truth or joy in your pain, you need not do so. I would never offer such a platitude to somebody who had just suffered the loss of a child or who had gone through the same cancer that I had. At some point, though, perhaps you may be in a place of healing where you can find the perspective to see a silver lining. If you are ready, explore your adversity for blessings or lessons. If you are not, you may simply wish to meditate on the visual image of a cloud with a silver lining.

Exercise: Find Yourself a Lucky Charm

We are superstitious creatures. Are things going well? Then don't change anything you are doing, because something you are doing must be right. Superstitions like this are started by recognizing patterns occurring on or around an event and ascribing meaning and connection to that event. Humans are wired to notice patterns, especially with regard to misfortune. There is a reason why the facial expression for disgust is so recognizable across cultures and even species. We've recognized a pattern of misfortune. We noticed that our fellow creatures expressed disgust whenever they ate something nasty. Since it might be toxic, we took this as a sign to avoid whatever they just ate.

Think about some positive superstitions, though, which can help you feel more powerful as you go. Just as an athlete might wear his lucky socks to every game, you can wear a lucky shirt to an important meeting with your boss, doctor, or lawyer. When I got bad news, I would change my clothes and wash the old clothes in which I heard the bad news, visualizing that bad news just washing right out of my life. Pay attention to the things that make you feel good and develop your own talismans for success. You might dig out a special piece of jewelry that helps you feel ready for battle whenever you have an especially important appointment. Sometimes I would wear my dad's old watch, even though it doesn't work anymore, for good luck. Find something you can wear or bring with you that always seems to bring you good luck.

Exercise: A Portrait of Your New Self

Even if one suffers an illness from birth, there is often a time before the true gravity of one's lot in life sinks in. For those with a surprise life trauma, the delineation between normal life and what comes after can be quite dramatic. I find myself remembering even unrelated matters in my life by the cancer marker, thinking, "Oh yeah, she got that bicycle before I got cancer, so she must have been under five years old." When one is newly diagnosed, the whiplash feeling of life coming to a screeching halt can make memories feel like a slap in the face.

As you move forward in your wellness, recognize any things in life that may never be the same way again. You will not be the same person after your trauma, but that is okay. You will become somebody who has grown, changed, and become different. The scars that occur in your body and in your mind will become just as much yours as any other body part or personality trait. Allow yourself to mourn your old life as much as you need, but please don't try to duplicate or repeat anything that is impossible.

This point in time is an opportunity to reinvent yourself. The core of who you are will always remain the same, but the circumstances in your life have changed so much that you can now let go of actions that no longer serve you and seek to embrace new hobbies and ideas. During or following a major life upheaval, you may find yourself feeling that your identity is fractured. Part of the time you may feel like one person, and part of the time you may feel like another person entirely, or like a person adrift without a defined role. Devote some spiritual exploration to what part of your core remains the same.

Draw a self-portrait of your ideal self. Don't worry about your physical appearance or health so much as the things with which you surround yourself. What are you wearing? What are you doing? Draw a circle around the portrait that represents yourself. Draw other circles outside of your circle that represent significant people in your life and connect lines to them labeling your relationships. Then, inside the circle, write the things that will always remain the same, such as your place on the family tree, your relationship with spirit, or life achievements that nobody can take away from you.

Meditation: Wisdom in Waiting

Don't push ahead with an incomplete version of what spirit wants you to be. Brief moments when your life feels like normal can be like landmines, blowing your progress to smithereens, if you do too much too soon. If you are asking for time off from some of your obligations, make sure that you ask for a lot more time than you think you'll need. If you are ready to return to some of your former duties or activities, give yourself plenty of time to work up to your former effort.

Think of this moment in time as a time of glorious change. You will need to wait before you can move forward, so make the best use of this waiting time that you can. Make plans and dreams, puzzle over any confusions or conflicts, and define your personal philosophy with more clarity. Not many people are given an opportunity to pause some aspects of life to puzzle out the rest. As long as you are being forced to stop and think, use the opportunity to turn inward. In meditation, visualize any impatience as something grasped tightly in both palms. Squeeze as hard as you can and then open your hands, palms up. Wait in meditation as long as you can stretch it today.

Chapter 4

J

THE BLACK DOG OF SADNESS

In this chapter of the book, sadness is characterized as a black dog for several reasons. First, to shy away from using the word *depression* in order to distinguish the deep and natural sadness of grief from clinical depression that may require psychiatric or therapeutic intervention. Second, the black dog is a symbol in mythology and folklore for sadness and death. Dogs can be ravenous and potentially dangerous while being simultaneously a symbol of loyalty. In the same way, sadness can turn into an almost parasitic hanger-on during the grief process.

In this chapter, you can visualize yourself as the black dog in your own myth. If you are in a hole, stop digging. Or you can choose to personify your sadness as the black dog if it helps you to compartmentalize and have compassion for the part of you that is feeling this way.

Sadness can be a good thing. In fact, let us take a moment to celebrate sadness. Again, the distinction is made between the authentic experience of a case of the blues and the equally valid but unhelpful experience of clinical depression that may need to be dealt with medically. Honest-to-goodness sadness is something we experience from infancy and cannot be fully eliminated from life, so there's no choice but to recognize the beauty of the blues. Convinced yet? Let's list a few activities that you can do to make the most of your glum mood.

First, spoil yourself. Sadness is a good excuse to turn the lights down low, put on your favorite music that enhances and flavors a sad mood, and perhaps cuddle with a pet, a loved one, or a fluffy blanket. Books and movies that bring on the tears can be paired with a sad mood, and, if your stomach feels up to it, ice cream is a good accompaniment. Consider reaching out to speak with a loved one about how you are feeling, if only to bond over your shared grief about this lousy situation. Finally, use this opportunity to create art in whatever forms call to you. Capitalize on your next sad moment and use it, rather than simply trying to banish it from your life.

HOW TO ASK FOR HELP AND HOW SADNESS AFFECTS RELATIONSHIPS, FAMILY, AND HOME LIFE

Seeking Internal Validation

Raise your hand if you tend to overthink things and make problems bigger than need be. Such complicated problems have a direct impact on our happiness. Health, one's past, family of origin, relationships, financial status, social status, and innumerable other variables are implicated in our ultimate enjoyment of life. However, we often come across people who are generally happy despite doing poorly on many fronts. They've found simple happiness. As complex as humans undoubtedly are, there's something delightfully simple about what we all hold in common and what we each hold dear. Most of us take delight in seeing a cute baby, kitten, or puppy. Many of us find joy in completing a simple puzzle or seeing beautiful art or natural scenery.

Just for today, pretend that you are a simple creature and you don't need to have health or wealth or the perfect relationship to be happy. Spend significant time looking at pictures of things that make you smile. Sit for a while and pet a kitty. Listen to upbeat music. Perhaps have a chat with somebody who makes you laugh. Don't waste time worrying about whether you're being productive or if you're just fooling yourself. Make a list of things that make you smile and spend at least thirty minutes a day enjoying those things.

Another thing that has a rejuvenating effect on the mind, body, and spirit is receiving support from people you respect. In fact, if nobody has told you yet today, let me be the first to say that I love you, you're doing a great job, and keep up the good work. Sadly, a protracted crisis has the unfortunate side effect of giving supporters a touch of fatigue. While you might initially find people rallying around you, over the span of months their attentions will naturally wander to other things going on in their lives, while your hunger for support and encouragement only increases.

The only sure-fire solution for getting the validation that you deserve is to be able to give that validation to yourself. You can be satisfied internally as if the support and encouragement were coming from the most respected people in your life. You may be a long way off from feeling validated by your own words, but today is a wonderful day to start building that rapport and trust with your own powerful mind. Before you state affirmations to yourself, reach out in prayer to your higher power or your higher self, asking to be suffused with power and authority. Then, say or write out your affirmations. Seek internal validation as often as possible.

The first thing that you need to do in order to have something on the other side of this low point in your life is to decide that there will be an upswing from that point. Meditate and pray upon what to anticipate or expect at this stage. You might be able to plan something toward which to work. If you can make no such plans, allow today to be a moment of opening yourself up to positive expectancy. Meditate or pray with your palms open and upward, symbolizing openness to positive change.

You Are Not a Burden

If there's one thing that nearly all survivors of trauma have in common, it's the feeling of being a burden on friends and family. There's something deeply wounding about seeing tears coming from the eyes of a loved one and knowing that your situation is the source of his or her emotional agony. You are not a burden to this world. How can such an authoritative statement be made about you with such authority without knowing the circumstances of your living situation?

Consider that our idea of whether or not a person can be burdensome says more about the surrounding culture than it does about any particular individual person. For example, in Western culture, independence is stressed from infancy, with parents often immediately placing a baby in its own bed or room and elders almost never residing with their adult children. In comparison, other cultures in the world co-sleep with their children, move their spouse in with their families upon marriage, and laugh at the idea of Westerners letting their babies feed themselves messily instead of enjoying the bonding time of spoon-feeding a toddler.

In your journal, write a list of intangible or spiritual gifts that you offer your loved ones; in other words, avoid defining your worth by material means or efforts. Write instead about companionship, a listening ear, loyalty, and love. Allowing others to share your burdens can be a helpful tool to aid your healing. At one point, I confided to a friend who had offered babysitting that I felt like I was declaring that my time was more important than hers if I let her make good on her offer. She told me that it was an honor to be an important person in my babies' childhood. Her answer made me realize that allowing people to help can be a gift to people who would otherwise feel helpless.

Try to imagine for a moment that helping you can be a gift to somebody else. Perhaps you know somebody in your life who died before you were able to say goodbye or who struggled in silence when you would have been able to offer some alleviation to suffering. Imagine how much joy it would have given you to be a part of the dramatic moments in the lives of such loved ones. Now, you should take time to make a short list of people who can be trusted with the precious gift of helping you during your darkest hours. Choose a person to bless with a request for help.

Feelings are an essential part of the human experience and are life-affirming. Even negative feelings, like sadness or anger, can be a way to bond with other people or to make great art. If tears come easily for you, go ahead and express those feelings.

If you're lucky enough to have someone whose shoulder you can cry upon, take advantage of your close relationship when you can. It can be good to have a good cry, especially if you are holding it all in. If you feel bad about crying, or otherwise expressing your emotions, here's a way to avoid feeling out of control: schedule yourself some time in the day to cry. I'm not kidding. Schedule yourself, say, twenty minutes to cry every day. That way, if you don't use twenty minutes crying, you'll feel like a success, instead of feeling like every tear falling is a personal failure. Make time to express your feelings each day, whether it is to a loved one or by yourself.

. . . .

It's okay to throw yourself a pity party,
but you should at least try to give yourself some
entertainment and refreshments.

. . . .

Not all days can be good days. There may be a time when you need to break down for a good long while and declare, "This sucks!" It's okay to throw yourself a pity party, but you should at least try to give yourself some entertainment and refreshments. If you find that you're having an unreasonably bad day, do your best to make it into a celebration. Order pizza or even give a gift to a loved one to see the joy on his or her face.

Perhaps you're not in a position right now to enjoy watching a five-year-old tearing gift-wrapped presents open with unabashed glee, but there are certainly things that you can do now to treat yourself. Order yourself some gifts, order some takeout food if you're able, or simply enjoy a guilty pleasure. If you need to pour out your heart out and tell yourself that you simply don't deserve all the negative nonsense that is going on in your life, shout it out to yourself and to spirit. Spirit can take any anger you need to throw skyward. Allow yourself a day when you don't have to act strong and positive.

Maintaining a Sense of Normalcy at Home

Your home is your own sacred space, blessed with your energy. If you want to set specific rules about topics of conversation in your own home, you certainly can. If you don't want people sharing information about current news, you can ask them to put their electronics and newspapers away. Likewise, you can certainly ask that people not talk about your problems while in your home, if even for a short while.

Try an experiment at home. For one entire day, only talk about normal, boring, everyday-life topics. Argue about the prices of produce in the supermarket or laugh at videos of cats. The things that occupy your attention today can be anything except the thoughts that are weighing heavily on everyone's heart. Declaring a break from talking about your suffering is not a matter of denial, but an active direction of attention. Make today a day of frivolous topics of conversation. Talk about anything under the sun except the elephant in the room.

Meditation: The Victim Triangle

A strange dynamic happens in couples, families, and other groups called the victim triangle. The victim triangle consists of three roles: victim, rescuer, and persecutor. With the way you are suffering right now, there is little doubt that you may sometimes feel like a victim of circumstance. You might notice people around you sometimes playing the role of rescuer, trying their hardest to make all your choices for you or make endless suggestions about how you can live your life. You may notice some playing the role of persecutor, telling you to toughen up, or perhaps persecuting the rescuers in your life. Oddly enough, people shift through these roles as if playing musical chairs, so you might take your own turn being a rescuer or a persecutor at different times throughout your crisis.

The only way to break free from the victim triangle is to refuse any of the roles that can be so toxic to relationships. If you are triggered by persecutors and rescuers in your life, set appropriate boundaries now. The triangle is also a symbol of Goddess energy, representing strength and stability through change. Build your own triangle of strength. You can be your own rescuer. No one need be persecuted or victimized. If you feel like you have been victimized by fate, it is because you are validly feeling pain. You do not need to cling to victimhood moving forward. Meditate upon the image of the triangle as a source of strength and divine feminine energy. Identify any rescuers, persecutors, or victims in your life and set healthy boundaries.

Exercise: Coping with Rejection

It can be devastating when a friend or family member leaves our lives just at the point when we have the most need for human connection. Some people don't directly reject us but may indirectly imply rejection by refusing to help or refusing to talk about difficult topics. As always, understand that the actions of others during times of great stress probably speak more about their own abilities to deal with difficulty than about you or your personality and self-worth.

If you find yourself rejected by others during this time, you may have little recourse but to let go. You certainly can reach out to communicate about problems, but first take the time to assess whether you are in the right headspace to devote significant time and energy to mending an unspecified problem that may have nothing to do with yourself. If you have plenty of resources for coping with strong emotions, by all means dive into the fray of fractured relationships. But, if you are struggling to keep afloat in your own life, create your own closure. If you need to say goodbye to somebody who has rejected you, create a ritual for closure. Consider writing a name on a piece of paper and burning it, asking spirit to carry your love upward with the smoke to the person who has departed your life.

Exercise: Forming New Friendships

By now, chances are that several friends have left your side, possibly inexplicably. Give yourself some time to mourn any friends who could not handle the sight of you in pain or the changes that have happened in either of your lives. The good news is you can make room in your life to regain some of the types of friendships that you have lost. If you're a little rusty at the game of making friends, remember that you can't just pick a random person and declare him or her to be your best friend like you might have done in your early years on planet Earth. Friendships have to pass through several stages. First, you become acquaintances, next you form friendships, and finally those friendships can progress to a stage that you consider close friendship.

Acquaintances can be formed through shared activities or groups, which may be difficult but not impossible during illness or injury. While in outpatient treatment for mental health reasons, a friend of mine made friends with the other patients in her program. She even became a coffee drinker by sharing coffee with friends in the program, which made it easy for her to ask, "Do you want to go for coffee again next week?" Moving friends to close friendship will take time and gradual self-disclosure. Make the decision to call people into your life who will be your new close friends. Weave a friendship bracelet for yourself that can be either elaborate or a simple braid. Choose colors that represent friendship to you, perhaps green for growth and pink or yellow for friendship. Wear the charm to attract friends into your life.

 ## HOW SADNESS AFFECTS WORK LIFE, PLANNING, AND LOGISTICS

Fatigue

Have you ever been so tired that you've had to really think through what the consequences would be if you just lay down on the floor of your grocery store to take a nap and refused to get up? If you can identify with this level of exhaustion, don't beat yourself up for it. Talk with your doctor about how to manage your fatigue. Long naps can actually be a no-no for adults, with thirty minutes being the ideal amount unless you have a medical condition that necessitates more sleep. Delegate some of your chores or family duties to people who have more energy, if possible. And, of course, make nighttime sleep a priority. Identify some more-energetic people who can help you. Find ways to forcibly inject your life with healthy sleep and healthy awake time.

Being an Adult Is Hard

My peers constantly joke about how being an adult or "adulting" is fraught with difficulty. Being an adult while going through a significant life challenge such as trauma, cancer, or divorce is adulting on hard mode. At the point in life when you want to simply lie back and be cared for like a baby, you are thrust into the most difficult life choices you might ever face with the full knowledge that the responsibility for your choices ultimately lies within yourself.

. . . .

Whenever possible, make difficult decisions ahead
of time instead of putting them off.

. . . .

Recall that you can always consult your higher self by visualizing yourself being cared for and feeling relaxed. Whenever possible, make difficult decisions ahead of time instead of putting them off. I can't tell you what a relief it was for me to hand my will and advanced directives over to the hospital, having written them out two years prior, without having to make those difficult decisions at the moment of diagnosis.

Finally, celebrate your own coming of age, if you have not done so already. Your life challenges have matured you. Find a way today to personally celebrate your womanhood or manhood with a simple ceremony or treat.

The Practice of Withdrawing for the Purpose of Returning

In times of overwhelm, you may want nothing more than to shut off your phone, lock all the doors, and be all alone for a week, a month, or more. Isolation can wreak its own havoc in your life. Consider the tarot card the Hermit, which depicts a wise sage alone in his thoughts, and yet he holds a lantern that can potentially be seen by others. If you want to enjoy a retreat into solitude, here are some tips to make the most of such a spiritual sojourn.

Plan your retreat in advance rather than throwing your hands up in the air in exasperation and declaring that you're now incommunicado. Set a start and end time for your retreat and let everyone close to you know that you intend to withdraw from everyday life and tell them when you plan to return. Designate somebody in your life as your spokesperson so that if people start reaching out to find out if you're okay, that person can cheerfully let them know that you are away and will return. If you are physically going somewhere to retreat from life, make sure to bring with you any spiritual inspiration you need, such as journaling materials, books, and ritual or meditation supplies. Set aside a day, a week, or more as your personal spiritual retreat time.

SELF-CARE AND SPIRITUALITY

Exercise: Vision Is Found on the Mountaintop; Inspiration Is Found in the Valley

Survivors are the best people. They tend to cut right through the small talk and speak openly about their greatest hopes and fears, the way that I wish everyone could. The perspective and zest for life gained through adversity is why so many survivors of cancer and traumatic incidents become motivational speakers. Certainly, we could develop the skills and aptitude to become visionary thinkers, even without having been through trauma. However, down in the depths of life's valleys we endure the hardships that allow us to gain the compassion and insight needed to help others as well as ourselves.

This journaling exercise will be about your views on life and the people around you during life's highs and lows. Draw an inverted bell curve, showing a valley surrounded by two mountain tops. The first mountain top represents your plans for the future before your current adversity. Write down what visions you had for yourself and for the world. Now, in the valley, write down what inspires you. What needs do you see in people you meet at the hospital or your lawyer's office, for example, who are hurting? You can draw more hills and valleys to represent previous points in your life or make a guess about what vision you'll have for the future at your life's next high point.

Don't Put Yourself Down

Negative thinking can have a snowball effect in which it can get bigger and encompass more of your life the longer it goes unchecked. Thus far, I've encouraged you to fully experience all of your emotions, regardless of how negative they may feel. It must be recognized, however, that negative thinking can be taken too far, so let's start exploring some of the differences. Note, first, that there's a difference between thoughts and feelings. It can be difficult to tell whether thoughts or feelings come first sometimes, because they can happen together nearly instantaneously. However, it's important to make the distinction between your thoughts or rationalizations about your experience versus the raw emotions you may feel. Feelings are always valid, and there's no such thing as experiencing a raw emotion wrongly, as long as you control your behaviors. Thoughts, however, can be right or wrong or anything in between.

It can be exhausting to police your thoughts, so here are a few tips. Start by identifying what emotion you are feeling. You can write down that emotion in your journal without judging it to try to figure out why you're feeling that way. It's okay to feel sad or angry, even with no reason behind the feeling at all. If you notice your thoughts running around and dwelling on the reasons behind negative emotions, this is when you leap into action to stop the stinking thinking. This can be as simple as visualizing a stop sign and as complex as replacing the negative thought with a positive one or with a meditation session.

A lifetime of valuing personal responsibility can be a bit of a problem when you beat yourself up over mistakes. While you know in your heart that everyone makes mistakes, you might hold yourself to a higher standard than others. You may even routinely call yourself stupid or an idiot for making a mistake. Make a conscious effort to curtail that behavior. Why? You are a powerful person and your words can make things manifest. If you call yourself stupid enough times, you are inviting more foolish behavior. If you then suffer from low self-esteem, it may seem impossible to think otherwise about yourself.

Turn to your spirituality for support when increasing your personal power. Some people think of themselves as children of the divine, while others believe that the divine spark resides in everyone. If you wouldn't call a deity or its offspring stupid, you certainly shouldn't use such words about yourself. If your habit of self-deprecation is deeply ingrained, you may have to correct yourself each time you accidentally put yourself down. Over time, you will put yourself down less. Correct yourself immediately if you use terrible language when describing yourself or your mistakes.

Our secular culture has trouble allowing people to have a serious spiritual crisis. A "mid-life" crisis is looked down upon in disdain, as if it is only something that a man who wants to buy a sports car or have a younger girlfriend should have. But in some cultures, a crisis is something that is necessary and even respectable for anyone and is something to be undertaken with sincere spiritual discipline. If you are in good health, go out in the woods and hold a vigil all night until the spirits speak to you and share with you their wisdom. As it is, you need only take on the correct frame of mind.

Let us imagine, for a moment, that we live in a culture in which others appreciate that you are going on a spiritual sojourn. Be unapologetic if you need to take time to yourself to read deeply into scriptures and spiritual literature or to meditate for days without speaking. You are responsible for nobody else's spiritual development but your own right now, in your vulnerable state, and nobody has the authority to tell you that you are doing things wrong. Hold your head up high if you are in crisis, because you deserve to allow yourself to be torn apart and reassembled right now.

The Pendulum Swing between Despair and Awakening

If you find yourself vacillating between emotional extremes, you're not alone. Realize that the journey through the grief process may look more like a spiral than a linear path. If you find yourself feeling accepting of your situation one day and then plunged into despair the next, you haven't failed to grow. Moments of extreme emotion may seem to last forever, but they are often short-lived. They tend to find a balance. The seasons have a lot to teach us about balance. The change of the light at the summer and winter solstices is drastic from day to day, while closer to the equinoxes the sunrise and sunset times do not shift with such dramatic speed.

Observe the seasonal cycles and the holidays that surround them as a means of comforting yourself that life does follow a pattern. Make use of your calendar. The winter solstice falls on or around December 21 and the summer solstice on or around June 21. The spring equinox is near March 21 and the fall equinox about September 21. You'll need to consult an almanac or the internet for the precise dates for any given year. On these days, notice how nature around you is responding to the times of extremes and of balance, respectively. Mark your calendar with the solstices and equinoxes. On those days, plan to observe nature near where you are.

Sometimes, sadness can surprise you long after you've felt healed from the loss. A birthday of a deceased loved one might bring up old feelings anew. A love song on the car radio might cause a widow to pull over and cry on the side of the highway. A man who lost a limb to amputation might feel incomplete for years after the loss. The cycle of life after loss is powerful and sometimes unpredictable. The first time cracking a smile and laughing after a long period of crying can feel alien and familiar at the same time.

· ·

*Sometimes, sadness can surprise you long after
you've felt healed from the loss.*

· ·

Many spiritual faith traditions build their myths around cycles. Gods and prophets die and come back to life. Reincarnation represents the continuance of life after death. If your faith tradition offers symbolic cycles of death and rebirth, dive deep into books or stories that help you make sense of the mysterious cycles of humanity and nature. If you don't yet have a faith tradition that resonates with you, look to nature for comforting cycles. You may have already marked the beginning of each season in your calendar, and now mark down each full moon as well, to observe how the cycles of your life and moods match the cycles of the moon. Record the full moons in your calendar and then journal about significant emotional events that correspond with the moon phases.

Journal Exercise: Gaining Perspective

With age comes perspective, and adversity sometimes hastens the spiritual age of a person. Whenever you find yourself thinking in extremes or unable to get out of your own head, seek out the perspective of somebody who is several years, or decades if possible, your senior. This exercise will be to look to your own life to find perspective. Imagine yourself going back to elementary school with the wisdom you have now. In what ways would your daily life be different? What actions would you choose?

In your journal, draw a timeline of your life, marking each decade or whatever divisions of the years make sense to you. At each significant point in your life, write down what was your greatest hope and what was your greatest fear. Notice how your perspective has changed over time. It may be impossible to know how you would react to your present life circumstance if you were older, but it is likely that your thoughts would be different. Hopefully you're accelerating your learning on your life's path.

Exercise: I Love Me

Self-hatred is an insidious destroyer of joy, working from the inside out to destroy one's ability to enjoy relationships, hobbies, and vocations. The only way that you can fight self-hatred is with self-love, so before you get to work, you'll have to address any barriers to self-love. I recognize that there may be some wounds that cannot be healed without therapy, but if you have no significant abuse or mental illness that would bar you from working on self-love, start by listing any thoughts that stop you from loving yourself.

Perhaps, for example, you believe that self-love is equated with conceit and narcissism. Or perhaps you still feel guilty about something you've done wrong in your life, and you feel that you haven't yet suffered enough consequences. Realize now that there's no way that you can hate yourself into being a better person, and that the compassionate people you admire probably have high self-esteem if they are able to influence the world the way they do. Today's homework was first given to me by a Haida storyteller, who says that she wraps herself in a hug every morning and every evening saying, "I love me." She recommended doing this homework for the rest of your life, as it can be the most challenging and rewarding thing you ever do. In bed tonight, hug yourself and say, "I love me." Do this every morning and evening from now on.

Exercise: Misfortunes Come in Threes

In mythology, bad things often come in threes. When one misfortune comes, it is often followed by two more in rapid succession, followed by peace or the end of the tale. This belief might sound stressful if you're always waiting for the other shoe to drop whenever anything bad happens; however, it can often offer relief and a sense of closure. I remember a superstition my dad held when leaving the house. If he forgot one thing, he always tried to think of two other things that he forgot at the house before turning the car around.

Our brains are wired to notice patterns so that we can avoid repeating mistakes in our lives. Unfortunately, this can lead us to spiral down a path of negative thinking that can result in believing that we're having a bad day at best and are cursed at worst. Try to take comfort in the rule of threes. If your situation is one big misfortune, think about two others that followed, came concurrently, or match your problem in intensity. Visualize placing the three of them in a box, then tying a bow around that box, and placing it on a shelf, symbolically closing that chapter in your life. Seal them up with a visualization or meditation and move forward having symbolically placed them behind you.

Meditation: Reflecting upon a Dark Time in Your Life

We each have no choice but to view everything that happens in life through the lens of our prior experiences. Small children cry over tiny problems because their current issues might indeed be the worst problem they've yet seen in their short lives. Adults, however, have probably had plenty of ups and downs that are more traumatic than spilling a glass of juice. Reflecting upon the sad moments in life can help us notice how times do change and things can get better.

Take a quiet moment to recall another sad time in your life. You can cry about it if you need to, but try to take in all the lessons that the experience had to offer. Recall exactly how you felt, mentally and physically. Remember the sights, sounds, and smells of that moment in your past. Think about which people were there to help you, if any. Ponder if there was anything that you would have done differently in that scenario or if there were any lessons that you can take away from your previous misfortune. Now, take a deep breath and banish that old memory from your mind. Open your eyes and look around you. Even though you're going through a hard time, notice if there is anything about your life that has improved from the sad time that you recollected. Life moves in cycles, and bad times don't last forever. Notice how each challenge in your life can shape you in a positive way.

Exercise: Honoring Those Who Have Gone Before

If you haven't yet done so, research the names of your ancestors or extend that search beyond the ones you already know. There is a lot you can do with that information in order to enhance your spiritual well-being. Honouring your ancestors is important because it helps you understand the grand context of the generations of love that brought you into being. Remembering those who are now dead also allows you a sense of peace in the hope that you too will be remembered. When you compare the span of generations to our short lifetimes, you tend not to stress too much about little things like parking tickets and household drama, since none of it will matter in a hundred years' time.

Choose a few ancestors to honor from your list or from among those you remember losing within your lifetime. Ideally, you'll have some mementos or photos that you can use to set up a small ancestral altar. Set out a glass of water and perhaps a small token amount of food that the ancestors would have liked to have eaten. Take time to sit and commune with them. Feel free to ask your ancestors for their aid in your healing. Create this ancestral altar and spend some time communing with it each day, whether that means meditating or leaving an offering of incense, food, or drink.

Exercise: Letting Go of Sadness Completely

Choosing to let go of sadness completely is a choice that you will need to make repeatedly throughout your life, even if the best comes to pass with regard to your health. Happiness, after all, is only partly good fortune and temperament, and much of the remainder of the complex happiness equation is choice. This spiritual exercise will symbolically claim the power from within your own mind. One of my favourite spiritual poems, by Gwen Thompson, reads in part, "When misfortune is enow, wear the blue star on thy brow."[1] Such a blue star with ancient origins can be two runes blended together to make a five-pointed star with a diamond in the center and the topmost point enclosed as a triangle. This symbol blends the runes *wunjo, berkanan,* and *ken* to represent joy from sorrow as transformed by love.

---

1. Rik Potter, *Walking a Magick Path* (self-published, Lulu.com, 2015), 66.

Blue Star Bindrune

You can create an artistic rendering of the blue star fashioned into a headband, mark the star on your forehead with makeup, or even invisibly draw it with a forefinger. As you draw this powerful bindrune, gaze into your own face in the mirror, seeing yourself marked strongly with the symbol. Hold your visualization in meditation for as long as possible, and then briefly visualize it again each time you look at yourself in the mirror for the remainder of your sorrows. Use a star meditation to evoke the power from within your own mind to banish sadness.

Chapter 5

J

CHOOSING ACCEPTANCE OF LIFE

At this point in the book, you've traveled through all the classical stages of grief. Don't worry if you don't feel anywhere through with your emotional journey to healing. Ideally, at this stage of your path, you've experienced an invigorating and life-affirming jumble of emotion. You've arrived at the point of your life in which there is no choice but to accept what has happened to you and what continues to happen to you going forward.

Much like the other feelings you've had, acceptance is not one that you have once and for all to display on your wall like an award or certificate. You will have to draw your mind back toward the tendency to accept your fate repeatedly in a process that philosophers have described as Stoic.

HOW TO ASK FOR HELP AND HOW ACCEPTANCE AFFECTS RELATIONSHIPS, FAMILY, AND HOME LIFE

Clearing Clutter

A cluttered home can test the limits of your patience, especially if you are housebound or struggling to keep up with housekeeping due to working several jobs or being crushed by sadness. You may have already begun to simplify your mental, emotional, and spiritual life, so simplifying your physical surroundings can be a constructive next step. Enlist in some help to declutter and organize your space in a way that makes sense while you are convalescing from your crisis.

Once you've found your trusted helpers who can help you move furniture and declutter, have them bring over a few boxes: one for garbage, one for recycling, one for donation, and one for storage for when you're possibly feeling better. Mark a date on your storage box for when you think you'll be able to re-evaluate the stuff. Simplify your living space, and then take some time to harmonize the space. If ritual, altar, or meditation space has become more prominent in your living space, allow yourself time to adjust to using the space differently. Finally, reflect on how your decluttering has freed up your mind and raised your spirits. You will need to regularly go through these cycles in order to keep your healing space clutter free. Simplify, harmonize, and reflect in the physical space where you spend most of your time.

Don't Pity Me

The week before her stroke, Caroline bumped into a car in the parking lot at her kid's school. Everyone saw. She didn't see any damage, so she drove away, somewhat embarrassed. The next day, the principal of the school asked her to contact the owner of the car because she had in fact made a rather large dent on that shiny new car. Afterward, she encountered some very judgmental glances from fellow parents who had heard about or seen the incident. After all, she was a hit-and-run driver! Later, after Caroline suffered a stroke and lost the use of her right arm, their looks of righteous indignation soon gave way to expressions of pity. Caroline was okay with it. She had come to accept that there would be changes in her relationship with others. At any rate, pity was preferable to distain.

The change in attitude toward her, though, wasn't really pity. It happened with that flash of insight when people connect with what is truly important in life. In that moment, when they saw her struggling with the aftermath of her stroke, they were forced to ponder what it might be like to leave their own kids too early.

Coming to a mental place of spiritual acceptance of your health and its effect on others means accepting the limitations of the people in your life, especially those who might disappoint you in your time of need. It's okay to ask for what you want and need, and it is certainly okay to be frustrated with people who do not honor their agreements or meet your expectations. But, after a time, when you've felt all the anger that you need to feel, it may be time to accept your loved ones back into your life with their flaws intact. Of course, I am not advocating that you force yourself to remain in close contact with people who are toxic to your well-being or abusive to you. However, if they have harmed you and remain unapologetic, you can still reconnect with loved ones while establishing and maintaining healthy boundaries.

It is important to make sure that you don't allow people a chance to victimize or disappoint you again if it made a big impact in your life. For example, if your sister repeatedly refused to drive you to your chemotherapy treatments or stood you up, forcing you to make alternative plans, acknowledge that the problem may be no one's fault. Perhaps your sister couldn't bear to see you with needles in your arms or was completely in denial about the help you needed. Regardless, if you want to keep her as a support person and she remains unrepentant, you'll need to quietly internally fire her from the job you gave her and instead simply enjoy the role in your life that she always played: that of sister and confidant. Explore your frustrations with others to decide whether you can keep them in your life, with boundaries, and then release them from any unrealistic expectations.

My Life Is Mine
If you haven't had kids by the time you're middle-aged, or sometimes even younger, people around you will start implying that you haven't really lived. No matter what your age, you might also be pressured to believe that being single is no way to live, and that being chosen to be a spouse is the pinnacle achievement of human relationships. If you're unmarried, there are those who will tell you that you just haven't found The One yet. But don't worry. You will (read: should) find someone who will complete you.

Nevertheless, you are not incomplete, and your life is not incomplete if you are not presently serving a spouse or children. Any life crisis might lead you to question what you have achieved in this life. My own young daughter was following in my ambitious footsteps by complaining that she hadn't yet done anything great in her lifetime. I told her the same thing that I want to tell you: you were amazing the day you were born. Now, allow yourself to have some agency in creating meaning in your life. Create a big mark on the world by warming the hearts of one or more other people. Or simply choose to gracefully return to the earth that bore you. All you really need do is live and die by your own values. What else should a life well lived be than that in which we've done the best we can? Give yourself permission to have lived a meaningful life so far.

· ·

What else should a life well lived be than that in which we've done the best we can? Give yourself permission to have lived a meaningful life so far.

· ·

Putting Others at Ease

When you are in crisis, it is not your job to put other people at ease. Psychologist Susan Silk shared her famous theory of how to share your feelings during a medical crisis: dump out, comfort in. Let me describe how her theory works.

Imagine that, whenever a person is in crisis, that person is in the center of a circle of loving family, friends, and community. Those closest to the person in crisis are part of their inner circle, their close family and best friends. Those in the outer circle, acquaintances and coworkers, are basically onlookers to the crisis.

When you are in crisis (and we all get our turn to have crises), you are allowed to emotionally "dump" on anyone you choose. It is not your responsibility to protect others from the pain that is naturally occurring in your life. Your inner circle, in turn, should dump their emotional worries out on people in the outer circle. Likewise, those in the outer circle should only share worries with their own friends, and not dump on you or your close family and friends. Everyone should, ideally, be passing comfort inward to you. Don't worry about protecting the feelings of others when talking about your crisis. Gently remind others to comfort you and to share their own worries with others.

Exercise: You Don't Have to Talk about Your Feelings

Often, one is encouraged to talk about their negative feelings in order to process through them, but this default way of thinking is not always the answer. Perhaps you have good reason not to talk to the friend who is pressing you to pour your heart out to him or her. You may have chosen to take a break from negative thinking, you may have already had a productive session of sharing with a therapist, or you may simply not want to put your fears into words. If you need to decline sharing your feelings, know that you don't need to give a long explanation or argue with the person who is trying to be your outlet.

In fact, even if you need an outlet for feelings, your outlet doesn't have to be a person, and your emotional expression doesn't have to be done with words. You can express yourself by hugging a pet, crying softly to yourself, creating a painting, writing a poem, or singing a song. Even if you're the type of person who loves to chat about your problems, it doesn't hurt to make sure that there are a few other forms of emotional expression in your toolbelt for when other people to whom you can vent are not immediately available. Explore a non-verbal form of self-expression. Vent some of your feelings in a way that doesn't involve another human being.

Exercise: Feeling the Freedom to Share Openly and Honestly

As you move toward acceptance, however much like a circle or a spiral your path may be, you will notice some pushback from people who are in other stages of grief of their own. Your family and friends may argue with you about your life choices or rejection of some of their opinions, and they may refuse to hear you out if you want to talk openly about your fears or even your plans, no matter how far off the worst-case scenario may be. For example, your mom might tune out or change the subject if you want to discuss your living will, or your best friend might not take no for an answer if you refuse her insistence that any marriage can be saved with hard work by one of the spouses.

Notice the signs if somebody is refusing to listen to your choices. Is the person constantly changing the subject when you talk about a difficult topic? Is someone in your life not respecting your boundaries? Recognize when somebody in your life is at their limit of understanding, and don't push them to take in more information than they can stomach at this stage in life. Write down what you'd like to say and seal up your letter in an envelope. You can give it to the person if necessary or simply stash the letter away for a better time. Don't choose to vent to people who aren't ready to hear difficult truths. Write down anything you need to say and save it for when those words truly need to be said.

Recruiting Others to Aid Your Acceptance

So far, the idea has been introduced that some people may not be at the same level of acceptance as you are, and you've been encouraged to wait until others match your level of acceptance. Now, we'll flip that technique around on its head and encourage you to find an acceptance mentor of sorts—or at least to steer your existing friends and family toward accepting your condition, the remedies, the unknowns, and the various outcomes. For acceptance mentors, you can recruit others to help you adjust to your situation when you feel you haven't fully accepted the new normal.

You have several options. You can reach out to somebody who is in a situation similar to yours, but perhaps further along. A woman embroiled in divorce might seek out divorcees who finalized their own years ago. I sought out cancer survivors who were a decade out from diagnosis or who were living with more advanced, metastatic disease. You can also speak plainly with people who are close to you, explaining that you want to reach a state of acceptance instead of fantasizing about a miracle. Ask your loved ones to structure their language to reflect your preferences when they are around you. Call your friends on their denial when you hear it in their voices and in plans for the future. Explain that you are not trying to be depressing or giving up on life, but rather accepting life as it is and as it will be, regardless of outcome.

HOW ACCEPTANCE AFFECTS WORK LIFE, PLANNING, AND LOGISTICS

This Is Happening

By now, you may be entirely done with the denial phase of your grief, and you spend less and less of your time telling yourself that tragedy isn't happening or curled up in a ball telling yourself no over and over again. It's okay if, every once in a while, you indulge in a little freak-out, but embrace the superpower of facing your life's problems head-on. If there is one personality benefit gained through surviving adversity, it's the ability to accept a tragic reality more quickly and smoothly than the average person your age. The only danger is in knowing too much for one's own good and second-guessing legal or medical experts while borrowing trouble from the future that does not yet exist. Pray for clarity and self-knowledge. The next time you are worrying about a worst-case scenario, ask yourself if you are looking at reality.

Dismissing thoughts and feelings is not normally lauded in our culture, and somebody who simply throws up their hands and says "whatever" as an answer to "What if?" is considered apathetic. However, the opposite of anxiety is not apathy. The opposite of extreme worry about things that you cannot control is simply acceptance, and dismissing worries is a perfectly acceptable method of coping.

You don't always have to explain or justify things to yourself before you can allow yourself to relax. If you already have such a strong faith in your higher power that you can turn all your worries over to God, you are certainly empowered with acceptance, but if you can't yet fully put all your faith into words, you can still benefit from dismissing irrational concerns. Whatever happens, so it shall be, and aside from all the things you're already doing to support your health, there's probably not much left over that is simply left up to chance. Allow yourself to throw up your hands and relieve yourself of any responsibilities that are not your own. Dismiss any worries without justifying the reason for not worrying to yourself. You may have to release your worries many times, but over time this process will become more automatic.

. . . .

Allow yourself to throw up your hands and relieve yourself of any responsibilities that are not your own.

. . . .

Stop Avoiding Solutions

In some cases, we avoid obvious solutions because we cycle back to denial, or we fear the future once those solutions are implemented. In some cases, concessions or accommodations that need to be made might feel like you're giving up spiritual solutions or that you are lacking in faith, when in fact you are not compromising your spirituality. Consider a person who refuses medical care out of the hope that faith healing will take place, ignoring the possibility that spirit could be working through the hands of the very doctors and nurses that want to render aid.

Notice any time that you choose the "natural" or "spiritual" approach instead of a mainstream one and think about how you might be able to blend the two. Take on a new approach to viewing even the unpleasant or worrying processes in life as a miracle from spirit. For example, if you are prescribed a hearing aid, don't wait for a sign that God wants you to take on a hearing aid as an excuse to avoid a worrying lifestyle change. Instead, think that each new treatment revelation could be an exciting sign from spirit.

Exercise: When to Problem-Solve and When to Adapt to Adversity

There are many different types of intelligence, and as we discover more about how different cultures view the world and solve problems, we learn more still about how there are different smart ways to approach challenges. One measure of intelligence is the means by which people solve problems, but I personally believe that the ability to adapt to adversity with grace can be seen as another form of intelligence. The difficulty that a smart and spiritual person faces when life pours out many challenges at once is whether to adapt to the change or whether to fight back and try all means necessary to work through the problem at hand. It would be wonderful if life fed us our problems one at a time and then gave us each a grace period to solve problems before another one came down the line. In the messy world of everyday life, you'll need to pick your battles.

As a journaling activity, make two columns to evaluate how you're dealing with problems in your life. In one column, write down problems that you're actively trying to battle. For example, if you're refusing to give up a job that you are in danger of losing, write down your employment as something you're battling every day. In the other column, write down problems that you're trying to simply live with instead of combat. For example, if you can't be bothered to conceal signs of sadness or illness whenever you leave the house, your appearance might be a problem that is not important enough to solve right now. Evaluate for yourself if you want to start to move a problem from one column to another. Be intentional about the problems you are choosing to solve and the challenges to which you would rather adapt.

Meditation: Accept Your New Life Roles

A change in life roles can be very jarring, especially if much of your identity is wrapped up in your roles. If you have transitioned out of your career or if you have shifted your home role from caregiver to that of being the person in care, sadness and confusion can quickly ensue. This exercise is designed to philosophically divorce your spiritual identity from that of any roles you have held in the past or, indeed, will hold in the future.

Seated or lying down comfortably, take a moment to observe your breathing without changing it in any way. Your breathing is different from how it was when you were a small child, but the person observing it has not changed. You are your true self, not your body. Open your eyes and observe your body with a nonjudgmental eye. You may have new scars and skin changes that you did not have for your entire life, but the person observing your body's changes remains the same. Close your eyes again and think about the inner observations you can make, such as your emotional landscape and your life roles. Your internal and external roles have changed, but your true self has not.

SELF-CARE AND SPIRITUALITY

Make Way for the Pause of the Divine

If you haven't prayed before or if you're a little rusty, there are a few basic steps for starting to use prayer as a conversation with spirit. The most important part of a conversation is allowing pause for the other person to talk too. Allowing a pause in your own life for the Divine to speak to you is beneficial for numerous reasons. First, you'll be able to start a conversational relationship with your higher power or higher self. Second, you'll be able to use moments of intentional spiritual pause to meditate and seek peace. Finally, you'll be able to find peace in any moment, whether it be the moments before falling asleep at night or in a waiting room.

Prayers can be simple and ad-lib or flowery memorized poetry. The basic idea is to name the entity to whom you are praying (or simply direct it to the universe), then list some of the attributes you could praise about that entity. Next, ask for what you need, using whatever timeline you decide, and then offer your thanks. Finally, pause and wait for a response to your prayer. Take the time while in spiritual repose to wait in silent and receptive meditation. You might hear an answer, see a sign or omen, or simply feel a sense of knowing in your heart. Take a break from talking to listen to the Divine in quiet conversation.

Exercise: Mailing Yourself a Letter

Anthony was a family friend of mine who discovered that he had the early stages of Alzheimer's disease. He was a college professor who prided himself on his intelligence, so the idea that his mind was "going" was a terrifying prospect. He decided to keep working as long as possible and to not tell his colleagues about the diagnosis. Keeping the secret about his problem was tearing him up inside. Though his wife offered her listening ear to him, he felt that writing down some of his thoughts and feelings about life would help. Rather than just start a journal, he decided to write letters to his future self. He hoped that, if his disease progression was slow, he'd be able to review these letters and feel good about how the worst-case scenario hadn't happened. If, however, his memory had gone downhill by the time he read the letters, Anthony hoped that the letters that contained stories from the past would jog his memory or at least elicit a smile.

I was able to experience the power of mailing myself a letter from a lush, verdant countryside at a spiritual retreat place called Harmony Hill. The retreat center was its own little paradise, despite it being a chill and rainy spring. There were several labyrinths for people to perform walking meditations, including one that was wheelchair accessible. There was spiritual art everywhere, and plenty of hiking trails, though some of us were unable to fully enjoy them due to frail health at the time. Participants enjoyed plenty of workshops facilitated by counselors. One exercise was to write a postcard to ourselves and mail it back home so that it would arrive in a week or so. I was on the cusp of surgery, so I knew that by the time I received the postcard, I would know whether the pathology results indicated that my chemotherapy had either been successful, partially successful, or had failed completely, which would potentially limit my survival to mere months.

I walked the grounds with my postcard, unable to think of what to write. I wasn't sure if I would be offering myself congratulations for beating cancer or gentle encouragement that I was still a survivor and a thriver despite welcoming death sooner that I would like. In one of the labyrinths, which few had walked due to the drizzly weather, a number of spiders had woken up for spring and created a beautiful cathedral of spiderwebs glittering with raindrops. I drew the vision of spiderwebs before me, wrote a poem, and sent my card. By the time I received it, I had heard the good news that my prognosis was good. Seeing the drawing and poem I wrote helped me realize how far I had come. Write yourself a letter that you will open in the future at a significant time. Allow both reading and writing the letter to be a joyful walk down memory lane.

Meditation: Endings

Some monks actually meditate while watching dead bodies decompose in order to come to terms with their own mortality, but that's a little too extreme for this book. This death meditation is an exercise that is much less scary but is designed to evoke a similar rational contemplation of the cycle of life and death. Ideally, you will be able to undertake this meditation in a forest with a thick natural layer of decaying leaf matter in the undergrowth, but it is okay if you can't be in such a location due to geography, weather, or health status. You will visualize the forest, using each one of your senses to entirely recreate the intricate web of nature that always balances life and death.

Get comfortable with the meditation, preferably lying down or seated. In your mind's eye, see an old growth forest with a thick canopy, teeming with life. Visualize the greenery and the small movements of animal and insect life. Hear the sounds of birds calling to each other in the treetops. Feel the spongy plant matter beneath your feet and smell the leaves. Know that any time an insect or anything else dies in this forest, it becomes part of the forest floor, where natural decomposers get to work turning what was once life into the raw materials needed for this ecosystem to continue flourishing. Meditate on death as a part of nature.

Exercise: A Ritual to Initiate Acceptance

This activity is an exercise designed to spiritually stimulate an attitude of acceptance through art. You'll be making a collage, so you'll need your journal, a few magazines that feature peoples' faces to use in a collage, glue, and scissors. You'll also need four rocks to mark the boundaries of a spiritual circle, symbolizing the creation of a world between the worlds in which anything can happen and in which you can create your own bubble of spiritual acceptance. If you're at home, you can mark these circle quarters with candles, but you can collect special stones to mark the four compass points around you in case you're in an environment that doesn't permit candles, such as a dorm room or hospital.

Make your workspace in the center of your four rocks marking the compass points. Call on your higher power, seeing the presence of spirit within your circle in your mind's eye. Draw into yourself the power of spirit, knowing that spirit is an infinite well of acceptance. Draw your face in your journal and then start to make a collage of your own face using facial features of others cut out from magazines. You know that these parts are not yourself, and yet you are forming a self-portrait. As you work, you can chant, "Whatever shall become of my life, I will always be myself." When you have completed the task, take down your circle and set your self-portrait by the mirror as a reminder of your intention. Perform this ritual with the intention of recognizing and accepting yourself in this fragmented life.

Exercise: Ritual to Integrate Acceptance into Your Being

This is a ritual intended to help you find true acceptance, but it is not designed to just pull acceptance from thin air. Unfortunately, there are no shortcuts through pain. Even if you love making magic and manifesting with energy, you'll be a competent magician when you train your emotions rather than sidestep or eliminate them. The problem with acceptance is that it is slippery, and it can slide right out of your grasp on a bad day.

The point of this ritual is to try to cement the acceptance you've found into your being and integrate it into your true self to make it last.

For this exercise, you'll need three shot glasses and a larger tumbler glass. Fill the three shot glasses with cold water. Your next step is to charge each of these glasses of water with acceptance energy. Hold each shot glass tight in your hands to warm the water with your body heat while calling into your mind a moment in time when you felt acceptance about your situation, acceptance into a community, or a deep sense of self-love and peace. When you have completed the meditation with each of the shot glasses, pour them together into the larger cup and drink the water. This ritual will make the moments of acceptance you have felt last longer.

Faith and Acceptance, Together at Last

Life's practical crises have a way of creating a spiritual crisis of faith as well. A crisis of faith can cause a corresponding sense of despondency that does nothing to aid healing. The good news is that you can tackle any crisis of faith and find a sense of stability and peace even if you never figure out all the answers to life and spirit. Start with a little journaling exercise to evaluate how your faith has changed, if at all, since your life changed forever. Rank your confidence and stability in your faith on average before and after your recent traumatic events. You can rate it on a number scale or just draw a face to indicate how you were feeling. Now, draw a face or a number rating to indicate how you feel now. Is your faith stronger, or have you become a deeper questioner? Neither yearning and seeking nor feeling content is a wrong answer.

If you feel a little lost in your faith, take steps to tackle your questions. Doubt is a good thing, and it will encourage your explorations. Write down a few questions that you feel confused or frustrated about right now, and then take to the books or to local spiritual mentors to seek answers to your questions. What would it take to clear up your questions, whether to make your faith stronger or to find a more suitable life philosophy?

· ·

Sometimes, your own brain can be your worst enemy when trying to come to a peaceful mental headspace once and for all.

· ·

Sometimes, your own brain can be your worst enemy when trying to come to a peaceful mental headspace once and for all. Even if you've found peace and acceptance one day, the next day you might find yourself spiraling back down into despair or even denial. This journal prompt is about recognizing the patterns in your thoughts and your barriers to experiencing a general sense of peace.

First, write down what sort of timing your downswings tend to have. Do you tend to get very anxious right before a meeting with a doctor, lawyer, or boss? Do you feel a creeping sense of dread during the night that you simply can't seem to replicate in the bold light of day? Instead of feeling shame about patterns in your thinking, capitalize on your resources during those times and find someone or something that can offer you comfort. If there is no time pattern to your emotions, you might find cognitive barriers, such as not feeling that you are a good person when you flounder in your emotions or not feeling like you deserve to be at peace. Remember, always, that you are a divine child of spirit and you deserve peace, but you are human as well and it is okay to struggle.

Chapter 6

♩

PICKING UP THE PIECES

Okay, you've gone through the stages of grief. What's next? By now, you might have felt more emotions in a few months than you usually do over the course of years. If you're very lucky, you may have enough information on your biggest problems to know whether your potential outcomes are good or bad. If you have the chance of success, you might still find that the paradise you were expecting after a crisis is a moving target. People around you will expect you to pretend like your problems never happened, and you might be dealing with internal or external scars that affect you every day.

There are many tools available to you as you restore your well-being to full inner health. In Western culture, we know that we can turn to medical care that is research science–based in order to prolong the length of a quality life as much as possible. There are also many social and spiritual tools at your disposal that can be leveraged as well, and these can be used in harmony with more mundane solutions if necessary. You don't have to swear off your therapists, doctors, and medicine to treat your trauma naturally, because there is no part of this planet that is not truly of nature.

If it's unlikely that life will ever go back to normal again, the work of living with your new normal has begun. It is a mixed blessing to know your potential outcomes due to medical science, legal counsel, or other professional wisdom. If you still don't know anything about your potential outcomes or even the root of your problem, the work of letting go and trying to find peace in uncertainty has begun. Each of these scenarios can contain both peace and suffering, so your own personal paradise is what you make of it.

PICKING UP THE PIECES IN RELATIONSHIPS, FAMILY, AND HOME LIFE

Relax into Life's Comforts

It's unfortunate that our society values work so much that basic comforts are often labeled as guilty pleasures. If you have been avoiding your guilty pleasures, you should make an effort to indulge in whatever hedonism you can find. Moderation is your watchword if any one of your biggest comforts could also be considered a vice. Beyond that, spoil yourself. Use your shopping budget to buy yourself something nice, like a fuzzy, warm new blanket. Eat those chocolates in moderation. Spend all day binge-watching trashy television or playing video games if you like.

Make a list in your journal of the guilty pleasures that make you feel comfortable. Write down the amount of time that you usually feel comfortable indulging in such activities and give yourself permission to devote more time to what comforts you, if appropriate. In some religions, people ask for the Divine to give forgiveness for naughty behaviour, but in this mild case I would suggest thanking spirit for a world in which these comforts exist and are accessible to you.

I've encouraged you to simplify and organize your space at home while gaining strength of mind, body, and spirit. Your home is one of your greatest tools for healing since you spend so much time in that space. You can enhance your home space by building small altars. For example, you can create a healing altar with stones and trinkets that remind you of health. Pay attention to the sounds and scents that you create in your home. Some people like to use healing essential oils: for example, use rosemary, oregano, frankincense, lavender, or lemon, depending on what scent you find the most pleasant.

Re-evaluating Your Relationships

In the aftermath of disastrous life circumstances, many of the people with whom you have relationships will want to pretend as if nothing ever happened, even if something has irrevocably changed. A few people will want to deal with the change in your relationship by parting ways, others by cementing your relationship officially. For those who want to ignore the things you've been through together, you'll need to be the one to compassionately but clearly communicate any serious changes in the relationship.

If somebody has not been there for you during the hardest parts of your life, confront that person calmly to explain your feelings. Of course, you can't change the past, so you will need to forgive that person if you want to continue the relationship at the same level of closeness. The point of communication is forgiveness, not reprimand. Be courageous but compassionate. Even if you have forgiven a person for not meeting your expectations during your illness, you will need to base your life on these new expectations from now on. Gently explain that your new boundaries are not a punishment. One of the gifts that comes from a life torn apart is seeing the limits your friends and families have.

Now that the dust has cleared, many of the friends and family who disappeared may give you a call, send you a message, stop by your home, or otherwise come back out of the woodwork. Existential questions may leap to mind: Was this person ever a real friend? Were my beliefs about this person a lie? And, most importantly, should I ever trust this person or let him or her back into my life at all?

* *

Be thankful for the people who have been
with you throughout, even if they did not
exactly meet expectations.

* *

Recognize that any misplaced trust that you had in a former friend speaks to your ability to love and trust, not to any flaws in your own character. Release and let go of any friends who are not there for you anymore. Be thankful for the people who have been with you throughout, even if they did not exactly meet expectations.

Losing friendships in droves can leave a person a little shy about forming new friendships. You wonder if there is something wrong with the kind of person in which you tend to place your trust. When people make overtures of friendship, knowing about a person's recent tragedy, those false friends might fall in a voyeuristic category. These people may become friends out of curiosity and leave the person's life just as quickly as they enter it once morbid curiosity is satisfied.

Consider: What if your new friends are, in fact, the answer to your prayers? What if the people who have newly entered your life are meant to heal you from the pain of those who have left it? What if you have recently gained some perspective and a newfound awareness of toxic or false friendship about which you were not aware before? Treat each of your new friends as if your higher power has sent him or her to you for a lesson, and do not withdraw unless you're certain that lesson is one about boundaries.

Be Influenced by the People Who Believe in You

As crisis tore some relationships asunder or allowed other relationships to drift away, you found out which people were your true friends. Chances are, your heart and soul hurt when you discovered that your true friends were not as numerous as you thought or not the individuals you expected. No wonder it feels like another crisis of faith. You put your faith in someone and believed he or she could rise to the task, and you were wrong. If you truly believe in someone who seems to abandon you, your entire belief system is shaken. I have good news for you: you're more influenced by the people who believe in you than the people in whom you believe. What that means is, the people who remain in your life, even if somebody has let you down, are those who are shaping you into the person you are becoming.

It can be painful and frightening to learn to trust other people again. You must start trusting others by learning to trust yourself again. After being wrong about someone's true nature, it can feel impossible to trust your own judgment again. Just remember that you are not always wrong, even if costly mistakes seem to cover your emotional horizon at present. Ask yourself if you are putting your trust in the right people, and listen to your gut answers, good or bad. Whom do you trust and why? Can you trust your own gut instincts? Write down your intuitions about the people who have been helping you lately, disregarding any of their mistakes that may be irrelevant.

Train Your Mind to Adapt to Any Circumstance

Some people might simply seem more resilient or adaptable than others. Lucky for you, resilience is a learned behavior. Some spiritual keys to adaptability in the face of change are faith, hope, and personal power. You should be able to ground and center yourself. Practice by going to a somewhat stressful location or by having a conversation that is slightly outside of your comfort zone and then practice grounding and centering yourself. Don't take on a challenge that is too big. The idea is to expose yourself gradually to situations that allow you to practice adapting with some degree of success.

Once you are in a situation that makes you feel a little stress, take note of how the stress feels in your body. Ground by creating that connection with the earth beneath your feet and visualizing an energy exchange with the earth that may help you ease away some of those jitters. Pay attention to your breathing and visualize yourself in your place on this planet or in the line of humanity with your ancestors before you and the next generation coming after you. You are here in this moment.

Calm is contagious. When a hostage negotiator is talking down a fugitive, or a police officer is trying to de-escalate a would-be bridge jumper, he doesn't use loud and commanding shouts. He knows that the best way to have a conversation with somebody who is extremely upset is to use a calm and quiet voice. If someone is yelling and screaming at you, a quiet voice will cause him or her to match your tone or to at least quiet down to hear what you are saying. This technique can help you deal with distraught friends or family members, but you can also use de-escalation on yourself by seeking out people who are calming influences.

Brainstorm a list of people who have an inner calm that is hard to ignore. Set some time to spend with a person who acts like your emotional anchor in the stormy seas of big feelings. Note that the people who you love the most won't necessarily be the most calming people in your life. If you always feel energized and laugh as hard as you can when you are around your best friend, it's okay to spend time with her, but for this exercise you're looking for people who level out your energy.

Support Groups

Richard had always been the type of person to flippantly dismiss mental illness as a personal weakness until he developed depression following his wife's death. He grew tired of feeling isolated and like a failure every time he had to take his psychiatric medications, so he decided to join a support group at his local branch of the National Alliance on Mental Illness. He soon found out that his peers were anything but weak. He learned that the face of mental illness isn't necessarily the madman from a horror movie. It was the support group, more so than even his psychiatrist, that gave him hope for the future.

The reason support groups are so vital is that professionals who spend every day working with the suffering might never have been on the other side of the desk, therapist's couch, or exam table. Some of the advice given by an excellent financial planner, lawyer, or doctor may be impractical, while people who share your situation may be able to offer you workable solutions. Getting to know other survivors of crises such as your own is empowering and can make you feel useful and helpful when you offer your own support in turn.

. . . .

Getting to know other survivors of crises such as your own is empowering and can make you feel useful and helpful when you offer your own support in turn.

. . . .

If you want to get involved with a support group, talk to the social worker at your local hospital. Investigate whether there is a support group in your local church, community recreational center, or even gym. If there are no local resources for a support group, seek one out online.

In your explorations, you may find some people who have the characteristics of good friends. So far, I've asked you to carefully evaluate friends for their ability to hold your words in their hearts without judgment. Now, we'll go a step further and see which of your friends would like to be called upon during your time of need. A good friend can be someone you have on hand when your therapist isn't available to talk you down from emotional upset. Find a person who can turn your mood around and who has the availability to talk to you at a moment's notice. Don't choose for this job the very busy friend who has several children and juggles two jobs. And don't choose anyone prone to gossip.

"Call anytime, day or night." Many say this, but few friends take them up on the offer. Perhaps you, like they, are worried about bothering a friend. If you have someone who has expressed availability to take your call anytime, press the person by asking, "Are you sure?" If a friend is there for you, go ahead and call in the favor by giving that person a call next time you are distressed, even if it is at a late or inconvenient hour. Then, assess how that friend did, and whether the person seemed pleased to be there for you.

Healing Hands

Throughout history, there has been a strong belief in hands-on healing in every culture. For those who believe that a spiritual energy runs throughout the body, there are small epicenters, vortices, or chakras located in the palms of the hands. There are two very popular forms of hands-on healing available in Western culture today. Therapeutic massage is widely available. I was able to have an oncological therapeutic masseuse who specialized in lymphatic drainage massage. She treated me several times a month, especially after surgery.

Another, spiritual form of hands-on healing is Reiki. Reiki is practiced by trained, attuned practitioners who visualize symbols while allowing Reiki energy to flow into your body. It is likely that you have a Reiki practitioner near you, but if not, you can receive Reiki energy at a distance, just without the benefit of healing touch. People were meant to experience loving touch, so if you live alone, you may find that you crave this interaction. At the very least, ask a friend or family member for a back rub, foot rub, or a simple hug. Find a resource for healing touch near you.

Exercise: Observe Which Relationships Have Changed for the Better

The unfortunate reality is that a crisis can change many close relationships in a way that can feel like yet another devastating loss. It is hard to see the silver lining when somebody who was your closest confidant now feels like an enemy or your best friend no longer speaks to you anymore. However, crisis can also pull people together and make the good side of good people shine the brightest. Chances are not enough people rose to the challenge, so count the people who did and send them your thanks.

For example, after finally cutting a toxic mother and ex-husband out of her life, a colleague of mine, who is a life coach, was able to better bond with her husband. Lana had been struggling with a rocky marriage due to issues stemming from her family history. After a dysfunctional childhood with abusive parents, she married an equally abusive first husband who was arrested after a horrific physical altercation during which Lana received a beating in front of her own children. Though she remarried a wonderful man, John, she found herself holding him at arm's length and not allowing him to get emotionally close to her, out of fear that she would be abused again. When Lana's ex-husband disappeared from her life, running from paying child support, Lana realized that her life had taken a turn for the better.

She took the opportunity to cut contact with the only abuser who was still in her life: her mother. When the dust settled, Lana was better able to connect with her husband and leave the life of a victim behind her.

In your journal, write the relationships in your life that have deepened, softened, or improved. Write a letter of thanks to one of the people who has been there for you and deliver it to that person or verbally express your gratitude in person.

Reframing Letting People Go as a Positive Experience for All

Letting go is a part of nature's cycles and human relationships. In autumn, watch the trees letting go of their leaves in preparation to continue their growth anew in the spring. We all know that we have to say goodbye to our elders just as we know that we will greet newborn babies in our communities. Letting go of friendships or other relationships that fade or go sour during times of crisis can feel unnatural, but that doesn't mean that the process of letting go is unnatural.

Releasing a person from your life can free you up to fill that role with a new person. That may not sound amazing, especially if you're missing someone. Like a toddler being told that she is going to be a big sister, our brains rebel against the unknown. It may be easier, at first, to think of the process of letting go as helping the other person live the life that he or she is choosing. My therapist once advised releasing a balloon with the person's name written on it. You may use a more ecologically friendly option, such as writing the name of the person on a leaf and dropping it in a river or other body of water. Symbolically release somebody from your past, to make room in both your lives for future relationships.

Meditation: When Lovable People Seem to Turn into Monsters

Perhaps you've seen it happen to yourself at times during moments of extreme pain and frustration. Your personality suddenly becomes not your own, and you uncharacteristically lash out at someone you love. Or you've seen it happen in someone else. A person who was once a close ally suddenly doesn't seem to care at all, becoming distant at best and becoming an enemy at worst. I have seen addiction turn the kindest people into selfish strangers. In times of crisis, life can become an us-versus-them, win-or-lose game because of the fear swirling around in your relationships. It is easy to split people into categories of good or evil. But in real life, nobody is perfect, and nobody is pure evil.

If you find yourself in turmoil in your relationships, try to resist the urge to decide that someone is all bad. You don't have to take abuse from toxic people, but the compassionate thing to do is either to make peace or let the person go. If you decide to make peace, visualize the person wrapped in love, and give yourself some space before making amends. If you decide to let the person go, try to maintain some degree of love and care even as you set your boundaries. Imagine cutting a cord that releases the person from continuing to engage with you.

PICKING UP THE PIECES IN WORK LIFE, PLANNING, AND LOGISTICS

Mourning Losses

The mourning process will continue unabated, even if your life has leveled out into a period of relative peace. It is natural to blame yourself, to feel overcome with the number of losses you've experienced in such close succession, and to feel emotionally unwell even if your body is in excellent health. Treat each of your losses as something worthy of being mourned. You can mourn through writing poetry, throwing flowers into a river, praying for peace, celebrating anniversaries of events, or lighting candles. If you are missing people who have left or died, consider donating to causes that they would have considered important. Find appropriate ways to continue to mourn your losses.

The mind can always be changed through lessons learned when limits are reached. At your lowest point during your journey, you may have decided that you've hit your breaking point. I was surprised at what seemed to break me. I had suspended my fortune-telling work because, although I had received the all-clear from cancer, my husband had now left me. Stunned by this turn of events, I told anyone who would listen, "Cancer didn't break me. This broke me." Later, after losing an important court battle in the subsequent divorce, I cried over the phone to my best friend. I said, "My inner light has gone out." My friend then stopped speaking to me. So, I had to ask myself what lessons could possibly be learned in the wake of these compounded losses. I received the answer: perspective.

After each dark night, a new morning dawned. Whenever I felt I was in spiritual crisis, the crisis was resolved by the appearance of my gods in dreams, visions, and words imprinted on my heart by the loved ones who stayed in my life, unyielding to its terrifying onslaughts. Your next step toward resilience should be to refuse to be broken. Speak aloud your refusal to be broken, whether you angrily scream it at your higher power or whisper it reassuringly to a loved one.

. . . .

Your next step toward resilience should
be to refuse to be broken.

. . . .

Being Resourceful

Resilience is a mysterious thing. Many people are helplessly crushed by circumstances beyond their control and suffer for years. Other people seem to bounce back and be happy regardless of health, financial, or relationship circumstances. Psychologists are still studying the keys to resilience. If I had to name the biggest key to my own success with resilience, it would be the fact that I am resourceful above all else. When pride, wilful ignorance, or inaction get in the way of finding help, a person will struggle longer with a problem. That's just a fact.

So many of the exercises in this book are dedicated to making you aware of how the people and environment around you can be used as resources for your inner and external healing. Becoming a resourceful person, however, may be a change that has to come from within. Therefore, rather than praying for problems to be removed or for solutions to fall in your lap, pray and meditate on gaining the resilience to be able to connect with the right resources and make use of them. Take time to pray for and meditate upon the resources at your disposal and to give thanks.

I Can Choose Peace

The problem for very spiritual people isn't always their connection with spirituality or their control over their own minds. The problem is to remember to use those spiritual tools when you're feeling overwhelmed or distraught. For example, prayer is one thing that instantly calms me down and slows my heartbeat. But, when I'm feeling very angry, scared, or sad, I rarely remember to take even five minutes to pray. I need to actively tell myself, "I can choose peace instead of this."

Yes, inner peace can be a choice. Inner peace is not always an option on the table, but peace is a choice more often than you may think. At the very least, it doesn't hurt to try to find a moment of peace in the storms of life. Your challenge is to remind yourself to choose peace when your mind or circumstances might point to anything but peace. Consider writing a reminder on notes that you can post in places that you go to when you are feeling stressed out. Remind yourself to seek peace in those stressful moments and places.

Double Down on Your Priorities in Life

If, at this stage in your journey, you still haven't gained enough energy to do everything you once did, you can dig deeper into some of the interests and priorities that you have kept. For example, if you are not yet ready to return to work after a crisis made you step away from your job, you can find new fulfilling things to do at home, such as creating arts and crafts with your family or planting seedlings for a garden. If you've been putting off travel until you are feeling better physically, talk with your medical team about how to take that trip of a lifetime now instead of later. If you have decided that your spirituality is the most important thing in your life, schedule time in your day every day to study, meditate, or pray.

Take time to re-evaluate your values and write down what your deepest values are in life at this very moment. Remember that your values can be expressed in different ways. So, if you wrote down *travel* as a value, you might really be valuing adventure or experiences with other cultures. Once you have a list of your current values, which may have changed in recent years, write down a list of activities you can do now that support those values. Take one small step toward your values today.

Don't Let Your Optimism Get the Better of You

Positive thinking is the goal of this book, but it must be tempered with the tools of logic and reason. If you find that you suffer from incurable optimism, don't overcorrect the problem by crushing your wildest hopes and dreams. Instead, find a rational person off whom you can bounce ideas, someone who will be understanding and gentle with you. And remember, before you start taking the ultimate herbal cure to whatever you have, run the idea by your doctor first to see what a logical mind has to say. If you find yourself getting your hopes up, appeal to those with rational minds and gentle demeanors.

Exercise: Expectancy

Expectations can quickly cause overwhelm or disappointment, and yet refusing to think about the future causes sadness and worry. What's a positive-thinking person to do? The solution to the problem of having high expectations is to have expectancy instead of expectations. Expectations are when you set your heart and mind on a specific outcome that might not come to pass. Expectancy is simply the hope, the feeling, and the faith that something good will happen. Something. Anything! The idea of expectancy is to release outcome while still having positive thinking.

Here's a quick meditation to release outcome. First, think of something you hope for but that you know might be an unrealistic expectation, like winning the lottery. Allow yourself to think the thoughts that usually get you excited about that expectation, such as imagining yourself spending your winnings. Now, pause and turn your attention inward, away from your visualization. Where do you feel the excitement and happiness in your body? How does the joy of anticipation feel emotionally? Are you smiling? Now, imagine releasing your expectation like a bird into the sky or a paper boat into a river. Allow yourself to sit in meditation without thought but keeping the sensation of expectancy in your body and emotions. Perform an expectancy meditation for any unreasonable expectations.

PICKING UP THE PIECES THROUGH SELF-CARE AND SPIRITUALITY

Psychotherapy and Counseling

Therapy can be intimidating for somebody who has never had it before. There is unfortunately a negative stigma associated with therapy and mental illness that is entirely undeserved and imposed upon people by society at large. First, there is no shame in needing a therapist, and second, plenty of mentally healthy people seek therapy when going through a valid life crisis such as the one you are now going through.

What's the difference between therapy and counseling? Therapy is provided by a therapist who is trained to treat specific problems. Counseling is not meant to diagnose or treat any problems and is simply a person trained to provide a listening ear. Often, spiritual counselors such as clergy members can provide counseling for free, and secular counselors can be found at very low cost. If you feel that your trauma has developed into a more serious mental health issue, a psychologist can be found to offer therapy. A psychiatrist can also offer psychotropic medications to help. Find resources for counseling near you, or program the number for a crisis help line into your phone for mental health emergencies.

Stoic Philosophy

Famous Stoic philosophers include Marcus Aurelius Antoninus, Epictetus, and Seneca. Ancient Stoics believed that everything that happened to you, even physical ailments and health problems, were external things. They concluded that a person's inner virtue was the only thing that could be labeled truly good or bad in life. These ancient philosophers were aware of how devastating trauma could be, but they consciously focused on how their internal attitude could sometimes be good even when their health, finances, or any other life metric was failing. People had the chance to be resilient after suffering, and it was the task of the great Stoic philosophers to figure out what manner of thinking allowed people to obtain emotional resiliency.

If you are not feeling particularly emotionally resilient, it is not your fault. Unlike other positive-thinking proponents, the Stoic philosophers believe that if you're not feeling a positive attitude, it's not because you're doing it wrong. Look toward your own intellectual logic and virtues for validation and a sense of peace. Essentially, the idea is that what is natural and logical is good, even if it might not feel amazing in the moment. React to any negative emotion with logic. Assure yourself that your essential nature is good and remind yourself of your virtues.

· ·

React to any negative emotion with logic.
Assure yourself that your essential nature is good
and remind yourself of your virtues.

· ·

Stoicism, though helpful in this situation, is not the only ancient wisdom that can bring you strength and peace. You can also read through the scriptures of world religions for quotes and perspectives that can support inner healing. Mythology and even fairy tales can offer symbolism that can be deeply significant. Many spiritual fads that are marketed toward people dealing with serious illness come and go, but such struggles have been going on throughout human history, so reach for words that have withstood the test of time.

If you'd like to get started with your explorations but are not sure where to begin, consider picking up a book on the myths handed down through the culture of your ancestors. Not only will you connect with the spirits of your ancestors through learning about their culture, but you may even discover a myth that speaks to you on a deep psychological level. Read through any ancient translations slowly. Consider reading such works aloud to help wrap your mind around any grammar and syntax challenges. Each time you finish a good story or essay, write down in your journal the gist of what you took away from the work. Read some work of an ancient philosopher or an old myth, and write down some bumper sticker wisdom that you gained from it.

Ministry Is the Condition of Your Heart

At a gathering of spiritual leaders, several Christian ministers had traveled from out of town to set up booths to promote their ministries. These booths celebrated how different people tried to meet the needs they saw in their communities. One person's ministry was a library of free books that traveled around in an old van owned by a church. Another person's ministry was to buy movie tickets for foster children to see their first movie in the cinema. One woman simply had a booth of prayer shawls that she had knitted by hand to give to cancer patients and sick children. As I ran my hands over her handiwork, I asked her what made her acts of kindness a ministry, as opposed to any other charity endeavor. She answered without pausing in her knitting, "Ministry is the condition of your heart." In that moment, I noticed that she had lost her eyesight. I saw that her arthritic fingers would one day be unable to knit another stitch, but I realized that her ministry would always continue.

If you were to decide to set up your own "ministry" in whatever faith tradition or spiritual presence you have, what population would you serve? What needs do you see in your community that speak to your heart? What blessings would you give to the world if the opportunity arose? Keep an eye out to the need in your community.

Spiritual perspective can also help you think about why you've been saddled with hardship. Many spiritual leaders have written that the challenges we take on in life are the result of our choices. The philosophy that you chose to be born into a life that includes deep pain may not resonate with you. After all, would you tell somebody who lost a child that he or she had somehow asked for such tragedy? However, in some circumstances, it can be empowering to consider that on some level you were designed to be up for the challenges in your life. When I was mugged, I told myself that perhaps, by being the unlucky target, I saved another person who would have been traumatized for life or completely bankrupted by the robbery. Spirit often sets you up for success, so you can lean on that faith if it helps you.

Regardless of whether you have the spiritual perspective that you chose this life, there are probably aspects of your life that you did choose. List your life choices. Take ownership of them in a way that feels empowering. For example, if you chose to spontaneously leave a negative housing situation before it got worse, embrace the decision as one that was supported from a place of proactive power within. Ask spirit for the strength to carry out your own powerful choices.

Art Therapy

Some hospitals, clinics, and psychotherapists offer art therapy. Art therapy can help you express your spiritual strength and your visualizations or simply express those feelings that you can't put into words. In one hospital, an art therapist had patients color pages from a coloring book that featured a labyrinth as a meditative practice. They could then take the paper labyrinth home in order to trace it with a finger to relax. Ask your social worker if there are any art therapy resources nearby.

If there are no art therapists that you can access, you will need to be your own art therapist. Consider what forms of artistic work bring you a sense of peace and well-being. There are many adult coloring books available that offer intricate challenges for the budding artist. If you enjoy expressing emotions through art, drawing is an affordable outlet, as are simple watercolors. Create art to calm yourself or to express your feelings.

A music therapy program ran once a month at my hospital. A trained music therapist would either perform music or allow patients and families to create their own music. I have one beautiful memory of my children dancing to harp music played by the therapist. Another time, I brought in a cheap fifteen-dollar ukulele, and the music therapist taught me how to compose a song myself.

If there are no music therapists near you, it can be simple enough to find music that allows you to feel the emotions you need to feel. You don't necessarily need to correct a bad mood with music. If you feel sad, put on a song with sad lyrics and cry your eyes out if necessary. You can create your own music, if you like. The music you create doesn't ever have to be performed by anyone but yourself and doesn't even need to sound good. If you just need to bang a drum angrily for a few minutes, go ahead.

If you would like to try spiritual dance for healing, even if you're not feeling well, here's my advice:

- If you can't stand, you can enjoy sacred movement while sitting. Either way, adding a scarf to your dance can help to add beauty and flow.

- Select relaxing, slow music.
- If you need to take breaks, do so.
- Dancing can be incredibly grounding, so as with any grounding exercise, take note of your energy level before and after to determine whether it's working and how long you should dance.

Prayer

Get specific with your prayers. Pray that your case will be on your lawyer or doctor's mind when she goes to sleep or wakes up. Pray that your resume will be on the top of the stack if you are applying for a job interview. When the time comes for an insurance adjuster to decide whether to cover your claim, pray that they look upon you with favor. You can pray from your heart, using words that you ad-lib, or you can write flowery poetry. Prayers can be written on sticky notes and posted on your vision board or altar. They can be whispered or sung as desired.

If you aren't quite sure what words to say in your prayers, it could be because you're not sure what results you want at this time. Tell yourself, "I don't know the answer here, but I know who does." Tell your higher power that "only you can meet this need." Ask for guidance, clarity, and wisdom if only to properly formulate tomorrow's prayers.

If you've prayed every day for your problem to be entirely removed and yet it remains, perhaps you should start thinking about how to live with your problem. It is hard to strike a delicate balance between being determined to work hard on finding solutions and banging your head against the wall. Likewise, you'll need to find a balance between learning to love your life the way it is and being apathetic in the face of a quality-of-life issue that can be improved.

If you are about to give up on a problem, take time first to meditate and pray on the matter. I'm pretty impulsive, so before I gave up any writing projects during my cancer treatment, I allowed myself a night to think about it. Before I slept, I prayed for a dream to give me a sign if I wasn't supposed to give up. No sign was received, so I wrote letters of resignation in the morning. If you are continuing to work on a problem that seems to be unsolvable at this point, you can use a similar method of asking for a sign or omen in your dreams. Sleep on any big decisions. Be sure to sort out which problems are to be solved and which are now just a part of your life's landscape.

Meditation Silence Is the True Message of Communion

Add a moment of silence at the end of your prayer in order to listen for an omen or sign in response from spirit. Being quiet is the true message of communion. Every conversation has periods of silence built in, as people take turns speaking to one another. Sometimes, however, the moment of silence can stretch into a period of comfortable quiet between the people involved, which is the mark of a good relationship. Quiet time spent with the Divine can be considered meditation.

For this meditation, you don't have to close your eyes or enter any kind of trance state. You should, however, attempt to promote silence. Turn off any devices that might distract you, and allow yourself to truly listen, inwardly and outwardly. Quiet your mind and allow any thoughts to rise and then float away. You can write down any thoughts that come to you that seem to be from spirit. Write down if you hear any sounds like the barking of a dog or the croak of a frog. Allow yourself to become attuned to the sounds that you might normally tune out and ignore during the day. Through the rest of the day, try to listen more than you speak and to avoid vain or foolish conversation. Write down anything you hear that seems to be a message for you, whether it be a profound statement from a friend or overheard song lyrics from a radio. You can use quiet meditation at any time to receive messages from spirit.

· ·

You can use quiet meditation at any time
to receive messages from spirit.

· ·

Meditation: Peeling Feelings

You've learned along your path that feelings can be mixed up or layered to cause confusion. If you're angry, for instance, anger can be hiding fear of boundaries being breached. If you are feeling shame, it might be mixed up with or covering deep sadness. The mixture of emotions is one reason why some people see rainbow or muddled auras, the colored energy field that surrounds living things. It is the aura that inspired this meditation that is designed to center you and help you discover your true feelings about a situation.

Sit or lie down in meditation in a place where you feel safe and, in your mind's eye, see yourself surrounded by many layers of energy. Check in with your emotions and see if you can tell how you feel. What does the energy look like or feel like to you? Where around your body is it most thick or thin? Is it opaque or translucent? What colors do you see? In your mind's eye, peel the outer layer of this rainbow aura to reveal another layer underneath. How does the next layer look different or similar? How do your emotions feel different or similar? Continue the exercise until you see and feel more clearly. When you are done, breathe and connect with the earth to establish a balance of energy. Any time you are having trouble determining your feelings, simply turn your attention to your aura.

Exercise: Freewriting and Channeling

Freewriting is a practice that can bring out your subconscious. By writing without aim or goal, writing down precisely what pops into your head, you can explore and begin to heal traumas that you might have otherwise suppressed. If you ever feel irritable without knowing why, consider trying freewriting. Freewriting can also be done in a trance state to attempt to write down messages from spirits or the divine. This type of free writing is called channeling or automatic writing.

To attempt automatic writing or freewriting, get plenty of paper and a pen that you know will work. Don't worry about penmanship or editing. Find a quiet place where you can be alone and uninterrupted. You can facilitate a trance state by meditating, playing soft music, or drumming. When you feel relaxed and open, begin to write without thought as to what words are going to come out on paper. After a time, ground yourself and review what you've written.

Exercise: Learning from Failure Is Optional

Experiencing failures in life is mandatory but learning a lesson from each of your failures is optional. Similarly, suffering through challenges that you don't deserve is another mandatory part of life, but being able to seek wisdom through your suffering is a bonus you'll need to work hard to achieve. Learning from hardship doesn't mean that you need to view every hardship as a gift or that you have to feel like everything is all sunshine and roses. Even the most difficult life challenges can simply bring the wisdom of perspective.

Draw a circle on a sheet of paper and write in the center of that circle the biggest pain or failure that you're experiencing right now. Draw a few more lines out to other circles, listing any of the lessons that you can learn. If one of those circles contains a lesson that is leading you to other wisdom, draw another connecting circle and expand the network of life lessons from there. Use this brainstorming exercise to discover wisdom you have gained.

Exercise: Confront and Release Trauma

Trauma from a crisis can seem to tear you apart, which is why some people perform a soul retrieval after an extreme crisis. The theory behind soul retrieval is that those fragmented parts of your soul are sometimes given away or lost: for example, when you make an agreement with someone to behave in a way that is not your true self. During soul retrieval, you take back those missing pieces and integrate them back into your being so that you can feel healed and whole. Some therapists and psychic practitioners perform soul retrievals for their clients, but here is a quick exercise that you can do for yourself.

Close your eyes and think back to a memory of a time when you felt fragmented. Ponder any decisions about yourself that you made during this time. For example, when you were diagnosed, you might have decided that you were doomed. Think back to that moment and take back that decision. In your mind's eye, look around for a symbol of your soul fragment. It might look like a piece of yourself, a jewel, or any other symbol. Take it back and let it merge with you, perhaps melting into your heart. Repeat the exercise until you feel a sense of relief and wholeness.

Exercise: Uncrossing Any Hexes or Curses on Your Life

Unfortunately, many people I know who have suffered protracted misfortunes believe that there is some sort of curse placed upon them. Spiritual people and intelligent people are more likely to have this concern, because they know that magic exists and is powerful and because they are more apt to pick up on subtle life patterns. The good news is that such curses from an external source are very rare. The bad news is that thinking and believing that you are cursed can actually begin to create its own bad luck, since our minds are so powerful. It does no harm to perform a quick unhexing, so here is one that you can perform yourself.

Take an offering of a white food, such as milk, an egg, or bread, to a three-way crossroads. If you are unable to travel, you may perform the blessing over the food at home or in the hospital and have a friend or family member deliver it to the crossroads. Before performing the blessing, temporarily untie any knots on your person, such as shoelaces or the ties on the back of a hospital gown. Pray over the offering, asking your higher power to remove any hex immediately, with harm to none. Give thanks and take a moment of silence to watch for any signs or omens. When you hand over the offering, clap your hands three times. It is done.

Exercise: Making a List of the Things That Are Heavy on Your Heart

A beautiful tradition from Guatemala is to own a set of worry dolls. Worry dolls are small dolls, usually made of cloth, string, and bits of wood, that are kept in a small bag. Before sleeping, one is supposed to tell one's worries to the dolls, and then place them underneath one's pillow. I have my own set of worry dolls, and I have made some of my own out of craft clothespins. They never completely remove my worries, but they hold them for me while I sleep.

I've encouraged you to put voice to your worries, since they often don't make as much sense when put into words as they do when they float around in your head as an amorphous source of dread. Write down each of the worries that weighs heavily on your heart during the day, long before bedtime. If you can do so, delegate any of your worries to real people who can take care of specific tasks for you. Write down on your calendar or to-do list any other problems that can be worked upon in the future. The rest can be placed on an altar or under your pillow for spirit or your higher self to process while you rest. Put your problems in writing in order to come up with a battle plan to solve them.

Chapter 7

J

GAINING STRENGTH, CONFIDENCE, AND HEALING

This section of the book was written for people who are gaining some momentum with their positive thinking and inner well-being. Again, you don't have to be facing a good outcome or have all your problems solved to experience inner healing and reclamation. By now, I hope that you've made a decision to live the best life you can, regardless of your circumstances. Whether your future holds good news or not, you're likely to need to repair some of the emotional damage caused by your initial trauma and the destruction that crisis can cause to relationships. At the same time, you'll have to continue on your problem-solving journey, since it's not over yet.

Everything in life is informed by your character. Allow this time to shape your character positively. What is spirit trying to shape in you? The sooner you shape that in yourself, instead of resisting, the sooner some drama in your life or in your heart may end. Identify the attributes that you find divinely inspired. Give yourself gifts, acknowledgments, and awards for displaying good character. Acknowledge what spirit is making work in you.

If you're not ready to begin a deeper level of inner work, you can repeat any exercises from this book that have helped you or look for subheadings that match what you're going through right now. If, however, you're ready to charge forward into getting some of your own strength back in whatever forms are available to you, roll up your sleeves and get started.

GAINING CONFIDENCE IN RELATIONSHIPS, FAMILY, AND HOME LIFE

Telling Your Story

There is only one person who can fully tell your story, and that is you. Why should you tell your story? You have become the hero in your own hero's journey. Just like children who sit around the feet of their elders to hear how a hero brought back magic beans, adults need heroes who journey through the dangers of our cultural mythos. Since you have survived more difficulty than some people have ever seen, they want to know more about you and what part of you gave you the mettle to succeed as you have thus far. People who have never faced problems such as yours might hang on your every word.

At the very least, you should consider journaling about the details of your current problems for your own benefit. There is no better way to see how far you've come than to read your past writings. You may also be surprised at how quickly the details fade, including which people helped you the most. If you'd like to share your story more widely, find your audience through a blog online or through speaking to others at schools and hospitals about your experience.

Telling Your Family Your Wishes and Needs

Nancy had a car accident that left her walking on crutches while caring for three young children. Her mother called, asking if she needed a little help around the house. Nancy told her that she was doing just fine. When the mom came for a regularly scheduled visit a couple of weeks later, she realized that Nancy was in rough shape and that she should have accepted her offer for help. She told Nancy that in the future, instead of asking if she needed help, she would ask, "Is it okay if I come over to help?" If you constantly struggle with asking for help, consider agreeing on a code word or phrase with your friends and relatives. As you are gaining strength, your special needs don't entirely disappear, and it can be easy for people to mistake your strength for invincibility. Ask for a little help and a lot more grace, if needed, from your family and friends.

If you're feeling ready to begin serving others in your community again, since volunteering was something you once loved to do, be careful not to overdo things. Remember that your thoughts and caring for the world alone bring light to this world, and if you can do nothing more than be a prayer warrior for others during this time, that is enough. If, however, you do feel ready to serve others more at this time, think twice before taking over your old roles in organizations if your energy level, mobility, or availability to help has significantly changed.

Look in your heart to see what population of people you'd like to help the most, as your perspective may have changed.

Choose one population of people to serve, and then reach out to a charity or organization with details about yourself and any challenges that may affect your ability to serve. You might be able to find a couple of hours a week of community service that you can do from home, such as stuffing envelopes or doing computer work. Remember to take small steps toward your goals and not to take on too much at once.

Helper personalities, or "lightworkers," often have trouble saying no. They may spend every day trying to improve the lives of others. When a stranger asks me for help, I usually can't bring myself to say no. It's because I worry that spirit has placed the person in need in my path specifically so that they can be helped. If I decline someone's request for aid, I feel the need to refer the person to somebody who can help them or to give a lengthy explanation for why I would usually help the person but cannot right now.

If you are low on energy, you must first reserve your own energy for your own reclamation. For example, there's a good reason I declined to donate blood right before my treatment started, even though I wouldn't be able to donate blood again for at least six years. I needed all that blood for myself. When you make the extra effort to explain yourself and apologise profusely, you are diminishing the very energy that you were trying to conserve. Practice saying no to requests for your energy and efforts, without additional excuses.

Allow Yourself to Be Inspiring

Hopefully, by now, at least one person has been brave enough to tell you that you have inspired him or her in some way. If you feel flummoxed by such praise, don't automatically dismiss the praise outright. Humility is a good thing, but that doesn't mean you should close yourself off entirely to the positive impact you can make on the world.

Two questions for your prayers and your journal are these: How am I an inspiration to others? How can I be more inspirational? The answers to these questions will be as individual as you are. You can certainly seek input from people who will give you honest answers, preferably those who have already told you that you are inspiring. Write down your ideas and give yourself permission to be great.

. . . .
How can today be an adventure?
. . . .

Every day is an adventure. What is the difference between an adventure and an ordinary day? Curiosity is one essential component of every adventure. When I approached the oncology ward for the first time, with my inspirational mug in hand, I tried to remain curious about chemotherapy, surgery, and radiation. I asked questions about the science and process behind treatment, rather than just closing my eyes and hoping it would all be over as soon as possible. Even after treatment, the attitude of adventure helps me view small challenges differently. Figuring out a bus route to a new place in a new city is now an adventure, instead of something I'd rather skip because it's hard. How can today be an adventure? How can your next visit to your doctor be an adventure? List a few curious questions you can discover yourself or learn from someone else on your next adventure.

My mother always says that when life stops being challenging, that's how you know you're dead. That statement may seem too depressing for a book about positivity, but you'd have to know my mother to fully understand the humor and hope that springs from pragmatism and perspective. My mom is an incurable optimist and is one of the most consistently cheerful people I know. I grew up understanding that a run of so-called bad luck did not mean that things in life are negative or that I was making the wrong choices. Life is naturally full of variance, including upswings and downswings. In fact, an afterlife of pure paradise is personally rather terrifying to me, because it means that I would never be able to learn or experience the sense of risk that can lead to love and other strongly positive emotions. As a result, I already believe that I am living in the best of all possible worlds.

Explore how your personal view of the afterlife compares to this world. Do you believe that, after this life, there will still be lessons to be learned? Will the afterlife still contain the contrasts of joy and strife, pleasure and pain? Is there a different, life-affirming perspective that you can make use of during your time here on earth during this lifetime? You don't have to know all the answers, as this thought exercise is meant to be a snapshot in time of your understanding.

GAINING STRENGTH FOR WORK LIFE, PLANNING, AND LOGISTICS

You Can Do It. Why Not You?

Remove your self-imposed barriers. You may be aware of the many barriers that already stand in your way to total recovery.

You don't have to think about those struggles all the time, however. Sometimes you can consider how much is going right for you and ask yourself, "Why not?" If it is possible for you to reclaim and rebuild your life, why not you? If it is possible for you to go out on the town instead of staying in as usual, why not? Don't automatically shoot down positive ideas that may perk up your life.

Find at least one point in the day when you can say yes when you might otherwise automatically tell yourself no. Remember that you have the support of your higher power, your ancestors, and any other friends or family who would love to see you succeed in living well with the time and strength that you possess. You might need to strike a balance between moderation and caution, or you might shift your attitude to one of limitless potential. Ask yourself, "Why not me?"

Celebrate How Far You've Come

There are many things to celebrate as long as you recognize every achievement or life stage as a cause for celebration. In my hospital's oncology unit, there was a special bell in the chemotherapy ward that each patient could ring after he or she finished the final round of chemotherapy in the treatment plan. There's another such bell in the radiation ward. After sixteen rounds of chemotherapy I rang one bell, and after thirty-six radiation treatments I rang the other. It wasn't a large celebration in that it didn't involve a feast, speeches, or a party, but each time I rang a bell it was a symbolic victory that was especially meaningful after staring longingly at those bells on the wall for months.

Acknowledge each tiny slice of goodness in life. Not every day can be a good day, but every single day can have the best moment in that day. Start the practice of writing the best moment of your day. You can create a new entry for your journal each day. Or start a new journal of just things for which you are thankful. If you are too overwhelmed right now to start a new daily habit, simply write down the best moment you had today. But you will find that over time the practice of writing down the day's best moment will help you start actively looking for a good moment in each day. This can have the positive effect of manifesting more good moments and training your brain to see the positives. What was the best (or least terrible) moment of your day today?

• •

You will find that over time the practice of writing down the day's best moment will help you start actively looking for a good moment in each day.

• •

Find a way to meaningfully partition your struggles into chunks that you can celebrate. If you are recovering from injury or illness and meeting physical milestones, celebrate each time you achieve a personal best. If your woes seem to be never-ending, celebrate every ten or hundred days of struggle, depending on what makes sense to you. You can plan a celebration with friends and family, or simply ring a bell that you keep on an altar that you see every day. Plan a celebration of your healing journey in a way that makes sense for you.

The Power of Play

Humans are playful creatures, and it is our natural inclination to find ways to play long into adulthood. Unfortunately, Western culture values work over play and will often label play as immature, unimportant, and a waste of time. Take a look at the negative stereotypes ascribed to people who like to play video games for hours at a time or those who enjoy role-playing games like Dungeons and Dragons. Child psychologists understand that children explore their fears and new life lessons through play, and there is no reason to think that adults don't continue that process when not restricted from doing so.

If you would like to add more playfulness to your life, begin by making play a priority. Schedule time in your week or day to play in the ways that you enjoy. For some people, play can mean sculpting clay or snow with no particular purpose, dressing up and displaying a fabulous collection of dolls, inviting a family member over for a game of chess, or inviting all your friends over for poker night. The mode of play is less important than the fact that you engage in some pleasurable activity that motivates you. Play a game today, with yourself or with others.

GAINING HEALING THROUGH SELF-CARE AND SPIRITUALITY

What It Means to Be Powerful

It can be terrifying to lose emotional or physical strength. No matter what your physical, emotional, or social power, your spiritual power can continue unabated and even grow. There are two major sources of unlimited power that you can tap into right now. The first is your higher power, which you can access through simple prayer or meditation. The second is the power of the earth, which you can channel into your body through grounding. Not only can you rid yourself of excess or negative energy through grounding, but you can also pull refreshing power up through your connection to the earth. You can connect to the earth through visualization or by removing socks and shoes to create a physical connection with the earth. With each breath, you can pull up energy from the earth that you can see in your mind's eye and feel as a sense of calm alertness. Ground yourself, pray, or meditate to grow your spiritual power.

Catching and Stopping Negative Self-Talk

When you are stuck in a loop of negative thinking, visualize a stop sign to arrest the loop of repeated negativity that so often becomes a pattern in human minds. Negative self-talk can be a more destructive animal than fears about your situation, which are often quite valid. Emotions are generally good, life-affirming things, even if they can hurt. However, there are two emotions that can be destructive over time. These are shame and, to a lesser extent, fear. Fear is going to be expected for your situation, but shame is something that is not productive and should be your spiritual target. As always, you are the beloved child of the Divine, so you can remove negative self-talk and replace it with something positive.

Catching negative self-talk can be more difficult than noticing a fearful inner monologue in action, because negative self-talk is more often a habit that has been learned over a lifetime. Enlist the help of somebody who spends a lot of time talking to you. Have them alert you if you say anything self-deprecating, even in jest. Replace each statement with a positive statement. For example, instead of "That was so stupid," you can say, "Everyone makes mistakes." Replace self-deprecating statements with neutral statements.

Finding Your Self-Worth

Any problem that requires a significant degree of help from others can leave a person feeling like a burden, which can spiral into a feeling of worthlessness. Nobody is worthless. If you have ever felt worthless yourself, try the thought experiment of projecting that thought onto somebody else to see how worth does not logically follow from health or independence. A newborn baby is not worthless, even though it is completely dependent on caregivers. An elder is not worthless, even if he or she has failing health.

Your own self-worth must be independent of your health status, your relationships, or your roles. For example, a person is not worth something just because she is a mother, a wife, and a sister. The woman in the preceding example has worth regardless of her roles and relationships, and that worth was with her from the day she was born. Think of yourself as a child of the Divine and recognize that your worthiness is both borne from and fed by your own connection with spirit. Consider writing an affirmation such as "I am enough" and posting it in a place where you will often see it. Try out an affirmation that states your self-worth in terms of your connection to spirit or another immutable characteristic of yourself.

Meditation and Mindfulness

Throughout this book simple meditations have been introduced for you to perform as exercises for specific purposes. Meditation itself is a tool that can be used for many jobs. Meditation can make you feel more spacey or more grounded, full of wisdom or empty of all thoughts, energized or relaxed, or many other states of being, depending on your technique and intention. Clearly, meditation is a versatile tool, so you can think of it as a spiritual Swiss Army knife. If you've struggled with meditation thus far, the best advice is to get back to basics by practicing quiet, receptive meditation daily until you feel comfortable.

Start a daily meditation practice by choosing a length of time that will guarantee success. If five minutes is too long for you, try one minute. If one minute is too long, try thirty seconds. Expand your time from there as you gain experience. Eliminate all sources of distraction and try your meditation time at different periods during the day to see whether you're a morning meditator or a night meditator or something in between. Start a daily meditation practice of a short length of time that you can expand each week.

. . . .

When you are mindful, you are centered, aware,
and inhabiting the present moment.

. . . .

Meditation and mindfulness are two terms often used together, but they are not the same thing. Mindfulness is a state of being through which you can experience your days. When you are mindful, you are centered, aware, and inhabiting the present moment. Meditation can inform your mindfulness, and mindfulness can inform your meditation. However, mindfulness is something that one can experience independently of meditation and carry with oneself throughout the day.

To be mindful, you can begin with observation. Observe how you feel physically and emotionally. Observe your breathing without trying to change it in any way. Take note of what you can detect with each of your senses. As with meditation, distracting thoughts are a barrier to achieving the target mental state. You'll need to gently bring your mind back to the present moment by allowing worries about the future or memories of the past to gently float away from you as if they belonged to someone else. Practice holding a state of mindfulness throughout the day.

You can use visualization as a tool for things like vision boards. I will tell you more about them later in this chapter. They are used to put together an idea of what you'd like your life to look like. Visualization can be used for a healing meditation in which you see yourself in your mind's eye as fully whole and healed. You also use visual images while grounding to manage your personal energy. I'd like to build on your visualization skills so that any and all of those applications will be more effective.

To increase the intensity of your visualizations, you simply need more practice. Some people are naturally visual learners and have an easier time of it. Others, including me, don't have natural visual spatial ability and must work at the task. Try visualizing the details of a room or outdoor space in which you are meditating. Then open your eyes to check your accuracy. Over time, you'll be able to feel like you are meditating in the deep woods even when the closest forest is kilometers away. Spend your meditation time practicing visualization. Try five minutes or more if you have worked up to that time.

Nature

Author Richard Louv coined the term *nature-deficit disorder* to explain the mood and health changes that occur when people, particularly children, don't get enough time outside. There are those who believe that people should spend time outside daily, regardless of weather conditions. My own children are Montessori educated, and educator Maria Montessori believed in outdoor time so much that my very young children were sent out in nearly every kind of weather. The exceptions were lightning storms or temperatures significantly below freezing. If your health can tolerate brief outdoor exposure, consider spending a little time outside each day.

Even if you live in the city, you will find life growing from sidewalk cracks and planted trees at regular intervals. What should you do with your time in nature? Breathe, observe, and allow the sights, sounds, and scents to relax and heal you. You might take a sketch pad with you or create a scrapbook for days when you are not feeling up to a nature walk.

Crystal Healing

Crystals are beautiful and can brighten your day even without your knowing their spiritual uses. There are many healing crystals. Choosing the perfect crystal for healing your particular situation may be beyond the scope of this book. I will, however, suggest a few common healing crystals, and some methods for using them. Amethyst is perhaps the most common crystal used for healing. Citrine can help you think positively while you are healing. Selenite and clear quartz can be used to enhance the effects of both of the aforementioned crystals and to help them work together.

Once you have procured your crystals of choice, you can use them in many different ways. You may place them on your altar, on your bedside table, or underneath your pillow. You can keep them in a pouch worn or carried on your person. I took several crystals with me every time I went to the hospital throughout my cancer treatment. Some people even place clean crystals in a tea strainer to soak in drinking water to infuse the water with healing.

Exercise: Spiritual Detoxing

Not to be confused with the fad diets that claim credit for the natural detoxing your liver provides, spiritual detoxing is an exercise that you can do twice a year or daily in order to banish negative energies from your body, mind, and soul. This exercise is a simple one to cleanse your aura, the natural field of spiritual energy that surrounds your physical form. Start by attempting to visualize your aura, in a process like the one you used during the peeling feelings exercise. You can try gazing at yourself in the mirror, or simply close your eyes and see your aura with your mind's eye. Take time to scan through your aura, looking for any darkness, cloudiness, or negative change in texture, tone, or hue that could signify stuck energy.

Run your hands lightly through your aura or along your skin, visually picking up any of the dark, muddy, or stuck energy and pressing it harmlessly into the ground or into a piece of furniture that touches the ground. In some folk practices, an egg is run lightly across the skin and then broken open at the end to indicate whether the negative energy is gone. You may, however, find that the eggs you buy from the grocery store are too uniform to tell any differences.

Exercise: Self-Care

As you gain strength and move along on your path toward rebuilding your life, self-care will become ever more important instead of less important. The more strength you gain, the more you will need to manage the time that you spend in necessary activities and helping others versus breaks to keep yourself as replenished as possible. It is better to plan ahead than to reach a crisis and suddenly realize that you can't live up to your own expectations.

Think of yourself as somebody who is deserving of your own care. If you are a caregiver such as a parent or the child of a person who is elderly or who has a disability, think about whether you would put that person through the same stress that you do to yourself. If you don't have experience as a caregiver, honour the sacred within yourself. If you had a shrine to your higher power, you would probably pamper that shrine with offerings of flowers and chocolate. You would gladly sweep that altar and keep it clean. Consider yourself as a shrine to the divine. Treat yourself to gifts and rest. Perform an act of self-care in which you hold yourself in a sense of reverence. Put regular acts of self-care into your schedule.

Don't justify unacceptable behavior; accept mistakes instead. You also don't have to defend yourself or justify yourself to anyone. Make choices about your responses, instead of automatically reacting with excuses or defensive behavior. Spirit is compassionate on the good days and the bad, so cultivate compassion for mistakes in yourself and others. Many spiritual traditions have the practice of baptisms or ablutions in order to wash away the pressure of past mistakes or the influence of the mistakes of others. This exercise is one in which you will physically and spiritually cleanse yourself. If possible, take a bath in hyssop blossoms or wash yourself with a rag soaked in a tea made of hyssop. If hyssop blossoms are not available, chamomile is an excellent substitute that is widely available. Add it to bathwater or a wash basin.

As you bathe yourself, wash starting from the crown of your head and finishing with the bottoms of your feet, paying special attention to your hands and feet, since they are the primary means of interacting with the world. As you bathe, visualize the water filled with the light of love and compassion, as if you are bathing in the light itself. Imagine any dark stains of self-doubt or blame being removed and flowing harmlessly down the drain.

Meditation: Battle Sword and Shield Exercise

One way some people frame adversity is to imagine that their higher power has chosen them to take on the mantle of the challenge. This exercise is based off a vision that a friend of mine had during a coven meditation session. In her vision, she saw a goddess hand her a sword and a shield. To our surprise and horror, she said that she dropped the sword and shield to run away. As you might imagine, the challenges in her life did not subside simply because she ran. She might have done better to take the goddess's blessing and protection as it was offered.

Sit in meditation and visualize yourself traveling to meet your higher power. Imagine walking through a door to the environment in which you can meet your higher power. Take a moment to visualize him or her in full glory. In your mind's eye, see your higher power offering you a shield and sword, symbols of his or her favor. If you are ready, take these blessings and examine them, feeling the weight of them in your hands and noticing any ornamentation. Carry these blessings back with you to your place of meditation. Visualize yourself being spiritually ready for any challenge.

Exercise: Visualize Recovery

This exercise will be to create a vision board. A vision board is a visual representation of the things that you want to manifest in your life. Most people create one out of poster paper or a trifold poster board plastered with a collage of magazine clippings. The idea is to create a visual representation of what life will look like after you've manifested what you want and then to meditate in front of your vision board or leave it somewhere where you will see it often.

Gather your materials and remember that your vision board should depict your life only when your self-reclamation is complete, not any of the rebuilding steps along the way. You can create different sections on your vision board. For example, if you want to travel when life settles down, clip out pictures of the scenery you'd like to see on your trips. You can have sections for career, family life, and anything else that is a priority for you. Create a vision board to visualize your life after recovery.

Exercise: Becoming Your Own Superhero

Philosopher and mythology expert Joseph Campbell wrote that we are each the hero of our own story, and that each stage of the hero's journey is marked by challenges and adventures that repeat themselves in myth and history. In popular culture, we absorb ourselves in stories of superheroes doing heroic deeds. When I started chemotherapy, a friend who makes cosplay costumes offered to create a superhero suit for me. I drew superhero characters anthropomorphizing each of my chemotherapy drugs. For example, since Taxol is based from the berries of a yew tree, I drew a powerful goddess figure with climbing vines on her body and roots for feet. In order to manifest the power that you'll need to keep surviving and thriving, let's do an exercise in which you characterize yourself as a superhero or anthropomorphize your treatment protocol.

Choose your superhero name and dress the part if you choose. Draw the character you wish to become in your journal. If you prefer the art of writing, you can write a fictional story in a universe in which you are the hero, and your challenges are enemies. Place the images or story in a place you will see often in the coming days, to remind you of the power you can manifest from within. Create your own superhero storyline in which you can manifest or defeat anything.

Chapter 8

♩

FINDING YOUR NEW NORMAL

You might notice an odd benefit of any major crisis. When your life is in upheaval, priorities become clearer. The pains of life are sharp and real, and minor troubles disappear. After the crisis is over, one can take joy in the delicious blandness of relative peace; however, silly problems creep back in and assert their false importance.

Not everyone going through a crisis has a spiritual awakening, so you shouldn't feel bad if there's absolutely nothing good so far that you've taken away from your tragedy. Yet we each have a choice whether to take away lessons from life or not, whether the circumstances that bring about the epiphany be good, bad, or neutral. Be intentional about acquiring or remembering your sense of perspective based on your experience. Any time a banal annoyance takes up your brain space, bring your mind back to what is truly important in life.

The final section of this book is designed to be read after the major inner healing has already happened or been initiated in your soul. Again, your true inner peace and successes are measures that can only be done by you, not by professionals. People with mental illness can experience peace and well-being. People with terminal cancer can experience peace and well-being. You can experience peace and well-being. If you've not yet tasted this peace, you might need to go back to earlier sections of this book to work through exercises that you've found the most helpful.

After some progress has taken place, you can easily feel like your life has become undone. Life can never be the same again. If you are doing physically well, you may feel pressure from people in your life, and from your pocketbook, to get right back to the way things were. But that may be impossible. If you have come to live with an unsolvable problem, you have your work cut out for you to discover a new way to thrive in your ever-changing life. You are a brilliant, beautiful star in this universe, and you have only just begun to shine. This final section of the book is devoted to relaxing into the next chapter of existence and releasing what has happened to you along the way.

FINDING YOUR NEW NORMAL IN RELATIONSHIPS, FAMILY, AND HOME LIFE

Building Walls, Tearing Them Down, and Building Them Up Again

Your journey will become a spiral instead of a linear path of healing. If you sometimes feel like you're spiraling downward, you're doing things right. Think of your emotional healing as breathing. Breathe in, spiral to new heights, breathe out, spiral inward and reflect. Your friends and family will notice changes in you as well, perhaps commenting when you reflect inwardly and seem to shut others out. You've likely suffered more than one blow to your self-confidence and are learning how to trust and whom to trust.

Work on visualizing your aura, as you did in the peeling feelings exercise and again in the spiritual detoxing exercise. For this exercise, observe how your aura naturally behaves when you are in the presence of other people. Does your aura become thicker, more opaque, or more vivid? Does your aura shrink and become less noticeable? You are in control of how you allow your energy to react around others, so experiment with being intentional about who you let into your bubble. Observe and journal about how your energy field behaves around the people who are in your life.

Loss and grief are two necessary components of the human condition, but they can also be two liars telling you that you won't ever again know joy. If you have moved through your grief to this point, you may be taking stock of what you have left and comparing yourself to the "you" who you were before all this mess. Some things may seem simpler than others to re-gain, such as a new job or new acquaintances. Other losses may seem irreplaceable, such as a soul mate or a body part lost to amputation. In the face of impossible goals, one sometimes will try to protect oneself by avoiding necessary risks.

Take steps to make room in your life for new beginnings. If you have been waiting to end a relationship, let this new chap-ter in your life be your incentive. If you lost a best friend, intro-duce yourself to a new acquaintance or make time for a budding friendship. If you can no longer play a beloved sport, try picking up a new hobby. This point in your life may be about letting go and also about starting over, as they often go hand in hand. Let go of what is holding you back and take the necessary risks to rebuild a new life.

Let All You Do Be for Seven Generations

"In every deliberation, we must consider the impact on the seventh generation." This saying is often attributed to the philosophy in "The Constitution of the Iroquois Nations: The Great Binding Law." For example, it will make an impact later on if a parent shows up for his or her kids' life events whenever possible. However, generational foresight is not limited to those with biological children.

When first thinking about how one's time here on earth affects the future, most people focus on harm reduction, and that's okay. Committing to waste reduction and recycling materials is one way to be compassionate to future generations. The way that you choose to impact the future through either a proactive attitude or through harm reduction will depend on what causes are important to you. Some people might choose to eat vegan for the sake of animals, while others might try to use less fossil fuels or help the downtrodden. Think big and think long-term. What causes speak to you? How can you help those causes for seven generations into the future, through harm-reduction or action?

Talk to Your Higher Power First, Then Others

The spiritual answers have existed deep within yourself this entire time. What a long and strange journey you have had thus far, only to come back to yourself in the end and have what you so desperately needed all along. Our world is built around seeking external validation in the form of money, power, relationships, belongings, addictions, and personal stories. You are a resourceful person, so you've rightly learned to reach out for knowledge and support. Now, you must balance yourself by being able to rely on spirit when all else fails and reflexively turn to spirit before allowing yourself the helplessness of not knowing what to do.

Try consulting your higher power before anyone else. Instead of calling your best friend for advice or asking your spouse for approval and validation, turn to your higher power and ask the divine source that question first. Make it a habit to consult your higher power before decisions or self-evaluation.

Exercise: Letting Down Your Guard

One day, soon enough, a strange thing will happen. You'll go through an hour, an afternoon, or a whole day without thinking once about the disaster that happened to you. How would you feel about forgetting about your biggest life problem for a day or a week? Of course, I'm not talking about forgetting your medications or your appointments, but rather forgetting to fret and no longer displaying heightened vigilance. If your answer to the above question is that you would feel guilty, you have some work to do. Surviving a specific problem doesn't condemn you to living the rest of your life focused on your bad luck.

This exercise will be to set up an energetic shield that can operate when you're not paying attention. Close your eyes and visualize the protective shield of energy that always exists around you. Almost everyone has a

natural energetic shield that might look, in your imag-
inings, like a bubble of light, a ring of fire, or something
else. Next, imagine your favorite animal or a fearsome
animal guarding your natural energy shield. You might
see three tough rottweilers or a mama bear. Hold the
visualization, then release it from your mind, allowing
you to feel a sense of safety that your animal guardian
provides for you, day and night. Perform an animal
guardian shield visualization to relieve yourself of the
duty of keeping up your own energetic shields all by
yourself.

FINDING YOUR NEW NORMAL IN WORK LIFE, PLANNING, AND LOGISTICS

Re-evaluating Your Vocation

Most of my friends who have experienced upheaval have changed
their careers. Some of my friends are now disabled. Others need
to make accommodations within their careers to do less work or
apply for less hours. Still others have chosen to change careers to
one that is less physically or mentally demanding, to avoid the
necessity of implementing such accommodations. Finally, there
are many who don't have any physical or mental difficulty with
their former career yet have spiritual and emotional problems
afterward. Perhaps they can no longer stomach a job where they
are required to give parking tickets to hospital patients. Or as
an insurance claims coordinator, they feel it is wrong to deny
health care treatment, having been on the receiving end. Perhaps making big money on the stock market has lost its luster,

and the person now feels a call toward teaching or becoming a minister.

Take a good hard look at your vocation and determine whether it still aligns with your spiritual and financial goals. Notice that the word *vocation* is used, because you probably have a vocation even if you don't have a job. Your vocation can be volunteer work or your role within your family as a caregiver. Whatever your vocation, you will need to evaluate it now in order to avoid a crisis over the change in your abilities or life direction. Spend time listing the pros and cons of your current vocation or brainstorming a list of other potential vocations if you have already detected a problem.

Just as older people who return to school have a different learning style than young college students, you'll need to make peace with a new level of productivity. Don't be frustrated with yourself. Some skills you might be able to train yourself to do again, while other skills will never quite reach their former level.

Pray for wisdom and clarity and then give yourself a baseline test on what skills you need to be productive. Take a week to just observe what level of productivity you have right now, with any issues at play. Remember to look at measurable results, such as number of pages or chapters read, number of words written, or another quantity. After a week, you have a baseline with which you can experiment by adding accommodations or practice. After a few weeks of stable productivity, work to make peace with your new level of productivity and plan your work based upon what you can do.

Setting Goals

Every great dream is achieved through setting goals and working hard to achieve your greatest hopes. Goal setting can be intimidating for some people, because failure is emotionally devastating. It is important, therefore, to set smart goals. A common mnemonic, SMART, helps define goals that are specific, measurable, attainable, realistic, and timely.

Of course, you know that the best goals are those that are realistic and attainable, in order to avoid disappointment. Setting a way that you can specifically measure your goal is also vital. It can be hard to measure a goal like "becoming happier" unless you set some way to measure that happiness, such as writing down that it was a good day in your journal three or more days a week. Finally, to make a goal timely, set a date in the future during which you will evaluate whether you've met your goal. Then set some more.

Keeping a daily journal is a wonderful way to work toward your goals. You can use your journal for thoughtful exercises that extend over a long period of time. Consider keeping a goal journal, if you don't already. It may seem overwhelming, especially if your problems cause exhaustion and brain fog. Bullet journaling is a simple solution for this, since you won't have to spend a burdensome amount of time doing your daily journaling.

You can make a simple bullet journal out of graph paper and create categories you can check off. For example, a simple mood bullet journal might have columns for feeling positive, negative, or neutral. Each day you bullet journal, write the date in a row and then check off your current feeling. You're done bullet journaling for the day! Now it's easy to track the trends that your moods show across time. You can create your own categories for bullet journaling depending on what you'd like to track in your own life. Create a bullet journal page to put into practice this month.

Use What You Have

At this point, you may be spending much of your mental time in the future, leaving plenty of room in your life for the good things to come, which is generally the right strategy to have. Nevertheless, hope for the future must always be tempered with a healthy acknowledgment of what you already have. For example, if you only have about two hours of active energy a day, you don't want to spend both hours working out at the gym, even if exercise will increase your energy in the long run. You will have to adequately assess what your resources are before dividing them into your various priorities.

Name one asset that you have at your disposal in the categories of physical, mental, and spiritual. For example, as a physical asset you might have a good immune system, the ability to walk reasonable distances, or a healthy appetite. At your mental disposal you might have creativity, determination, and resourcefulness. Spiritually, you might have faith, a connection with your own spiritual energy, and fellowship with peers. Meditate upon how you can leverage your gifts right now.

. . . .

Even a person who has no major issues won't be able to tackle all their goals at once. If you are reclaiming and rebuilding your life, you will have some good days and some bad days.

. . . .

Many twelve-step recovery groups use the slogan "one day at a time" and for good reason. Those who take on too much time at once are not making smart goals, as their goals do not have any sort of realistic timeframe. Even a person who has no major issues won't be able to tackle all their goals at once. If you are reclaiming and rebuilding your life, you will have some good days and some bad days.

Live each day one day at a time by assessing each day as it comes. Use your body check-in meditation each morning to plan your day based on how your day feels. This week, try setting weekly goals rather than daily goals. Weekly goals allow for a day or two of less productive rest, while still getting the necessary chores and tasks completed. Try assessing your energy level each day for a week while working on your weekly goals. If you don't succeed, try reducing your goals the following week.

Exercise: Oh No, Not Again...

Nothing derails a winning streak in life like the news that things could be going back to square one. It turns out that cancer patients have been shown to suffer genuine post-traumatic stress disorder after treatments. Other life tragedies, such as divorce, create similar trauma. No matter how far you've come from your worst days, there may be moments that trigger a feeling that everything is happening all over again. I've included the dip back into low feelings in the acceptance section of this book because the spiritual work you do now will help you be in a position of strength when negative triggers occur.

For this exercise, you'll make a protection charm to ward away negativity. Create your protection charm in a safe place. Try carving or burning the rune *algiz* on a small piece of wood, but you can draw it on paper or use a symbol that makes sense to you.

Algiz Rune

The point is to create the charm at a time when you feel safe and calm. Then, test your charm by taking it with you to a place that might trigger fearful feelings. After successfully using your charm through gradual exposure to your fears, you'll be ready to use it in any challenges that lie ahead.

FINDING YOUR NEW NORMAL IN SELF-CARE AND SPIRITUALITY

Meditation: Belong to Your Higher Power, Belong to Yourself

One day, you woke up and you didn't feel needed. You didn't feel like there was anywhere you belonged. Do you wish that you could go anywhere and be comfortable in your own skin? Becoming a part of your higher power is one way to always be valuable. After all, if you think of yourself as divine or as a precious part of the divine, it becomes less possible to internally tear yourself down with negative self-talk.

For this exercise, visualize yourself in the mirror wearing a crown that marks you as a sacred person. Before going forth on your day, place your hands around yourself and say, "Everything between these two hands belongs to my higher power." If you discover negative self-talk, defend yourself as if you were defending a friend of your higher power against the verbal onslaughts of a fearful or angry detractor. Make it a habit to consult your higher power before decisions or self-evaluation.

Exercise: Body Scan

Wellness is a moving target. One of the biggest problems with getting your life to a new normal is that the new normal will continue to change. Your baseline ability to pay attention, exercise, or do much of anything changes over time. Everyone's ability to do things changes slowly with age, but for those of us who are managing after a significant illness, injury or trauma, some changes may occur faster. My fellow young cancer survivors and I often complain that cancer seems to have aged us significantly.

Practice checking in with your body regularly, with love and compassion. Each morning, as you greet the day, close your eyes and be still for a moment. In your mind's eye, scan your body. If you feel any pain, the symptoms of an oncoming virus, or if you see in your mind's eye any significant changes in your body's internal energy pattern, take note. Write down any observations in your journal, and then plan your day. For example, if you're coming down with a cold, you might need to stay home today. Perform a mental body scan in the morning to determine today's level of wellness and activity.

Letting Go of Unhealthy Coping Mechanisms and Substances

Throughout the peak of your crisis, you probably picked up a few unhealthy coping mechanisms. It's okay. Nasty behaviours that you may have used to protect yourself while you felt fragile do not mean that you're a bad person. You might feel like you are not as wonderful a person as you were before, because the cultural narrative tells you that survivors of trauma are strong, beautiful spirits filled with joy and light. In real life, we're all flawed people, just like everybody else. Some of the very personality traits that you used to survive great challenges might make for challenging interpersonal relationships once you find your new normal.

. . . .

Some of the very personality traits that you used to survive great challenges might make for challenging interpersonal relationships once you find your new normal.

. . . .

Pretend that you're introducing you to yourself for the first time and make a list of any perceived shortcomings in your journal. Carefully evaluate whether some of your old personality traits still apply. For example, I used to be a quitter, but now I have learned determination, so that shortcoming no longer applies. On the downside, I used to be more carefree, and I am now more of a worrier. Survey your list and circle those that you are willing now to give up. List any new challenging behaviors you have developed via stress that you'd like to reduce.

Exercise: Find Joy When Happiness Isn't Enough

This exercise is the counterpoint to finding the tiny bits of happiness in everyday life, for when that first cup of tea in the morning just isn't enough to override a deeper sense of unhappiness at your situation. Bear with me here as I explain something that is counterintuitive. Sometimes a thing can bring a deeply fulfilling joy while still not necessarily boosting daily happiness, and that's okay. Parenting is a concrete example of something that brings both joy and strife. It is generally known that parents rate their daily experiences of happiness lower than people who do not have kids. Yet some of those same parents will choose to have more children. Why is that? There are joys that make up for the unhappiness, and your task is to find out what those joys are for you.

For this brainstorming session, draw a circle in your journal and think up something that brings you a great deal of joy or fulfillment in life, even if it doesn't bring you happiness on a daily basis. See if you can think of related joys and draw other circles, connecting them with lines to the main circle. If you think of an unrelated joy, draw its own connections to other circles. Brainstorm the joys in your life that make up for the bad days.

Meditation: Radiating Your Positive Energy

Think of your positive energy as a service to the world. You can be a beacon of light. Here are a couple of tips for my favorite method, channeling. Channeling is when you act as a conduit between the worlds. This exercise is to channel the Divine through you and out into the world. Depending on your own belief system, and whether you think spirit is immanent or transcendent, you can think of evoking the Divine from within or invoking the Divine from sacred space.

First, let's try some transmission meditation. During transmission meditation, you say a short invoking prayer, speaking from the heart and asking your higher power to bring forth positive energy into the world. Sit in meditation for as long as you can, focusing on the spot in the middle of your forehead between your eyes. When your attention drops, in your mind you can say the word *om*. Second, you can carry crystals with you to help you radiate your positive energy from within. Quartz is a good standby crystal for the purposes of channeling energy. You can also carry variants such as rose quartz for loving energy, amethyst for healing energy, or tiger's eye for strength. Radiate positive energy into the world from within.

McCue, Kathleen, and Ron Bonn. *How to Help Children Through a Parent's Serious Illness.* New York: St. Martin's Press, 2011.

Potter, Rik. *Walking a Magick Path.* Self-published, Lulu.com, 2015.

Turner, Kelly. *Radical Remission: Surviving Cancer Against All Odds.* New York: HarperCollins, 2014.

Zimberoff, Diane. *Breaking Free from the Victim Trap: Reclaiming Your Personal Power.* Rev. ed. Issaquah, WA: Wellness Press, 2011.

To Write to the Author

If you wish to contact the author or would like more information about this book, please write to the author in care of Llewellyn Worldwide, and we will forward your request. Both the author and the publisher appreciate hearing from you and learning of your enjoyment of this book and how it has helped you. Llewellyn Worldwide cannot guarantee that every letter written to the author can be answered, but all will be forwarded. Please write to:

Alexandra Chauran
℅ Llewellyn Worldwide
2143 Wooddale Drive
Woodbury, MN 55125-2989

Please enclose a self-addressed stamped envelope for reply, or $1.00 to cover costs. If outside the USA, enclose an international postal reply coupon.

Many of Llewellyn's authors have websites with additional information and resources. For more information, please visit our website at http://www.llewellyn.com.